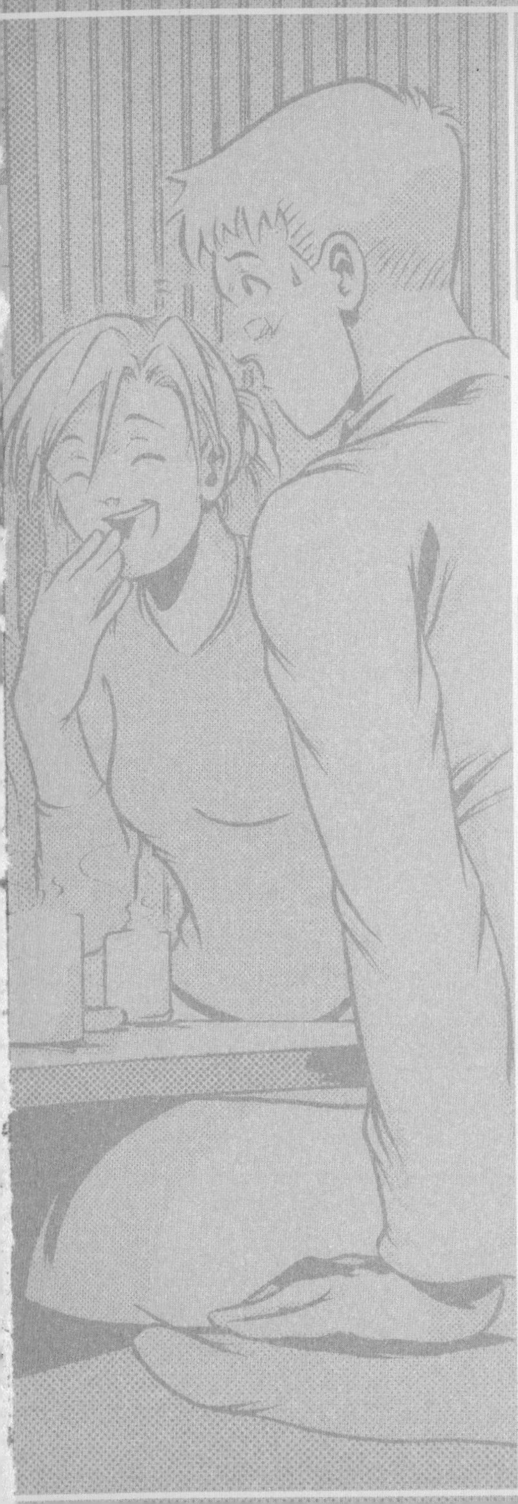

LOVE AS A FOREIGN LANGUAGE

VOLUME 3

Written by
J. TORRES

Illustrated by
ERIC KIM

Tone assistance by
NICOLAS GARDEAZABAL

Designed by
KEITH WOOD

Korean Translator/Consultant
HYE-YOUNG IM

Edited by
JAMES LUCAS JONES

Published by Oni Press, Inc.

publisher
JOE NOZEMACK

managing editor
RANDAL C. JARRELL

director of marketing and sales
MARYANNE SNELL

ONI PRESS, INC.
1305 SE Martin Luther King Blvd.
Suite A
Portland, OR 97214
USA

www.onipress.com
www.jtorresonline.com
www.inkskratch.com

First edition: June 2005
ISBN 1-932664-18-1

1 3 5 7 9 10 8 6 4 2
PRINTED IN CANADA.

Chapter 9

GOOD NIGHT, MOON-OH

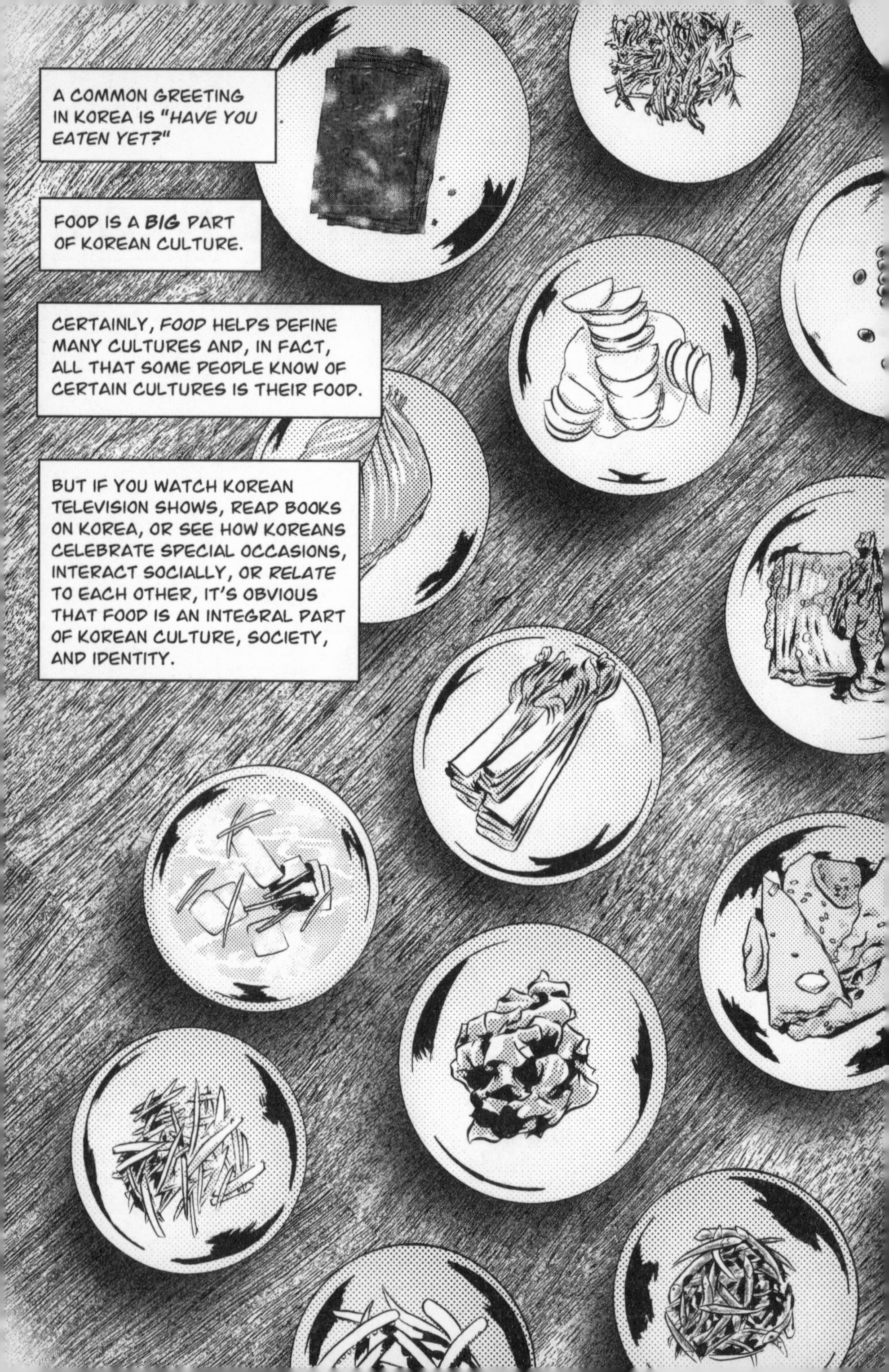
A COMMON GREETING IN KOREA IS "HAVE YOU EATEN YET?"
FOOD IS A *BIG* PART OF KOREAN CULTURE.
CERTAINLY, *FOOD* HELPS DEFINE MANY CULTURES AND, IN FACT, ALL THAT SOME PEOPLE KNOW OF CERTAIN CULTURES IS THEIR FOOD.
BUT IF YOU WATCH KOREAN TELEVISION SHOWS, READ BOOKS ON KOREA, OR SEE HOW KOREANS CELEBRATE SPECIAL OCCASIONS, INTERACT SOCIALLY, OR RELATE TO EACH OTHER, IT'S OBVIOUS THAT FOOD IS AN INTEGRAL PART OF KOREAN CULTURE, SOCIETY, AND IDENTITY.

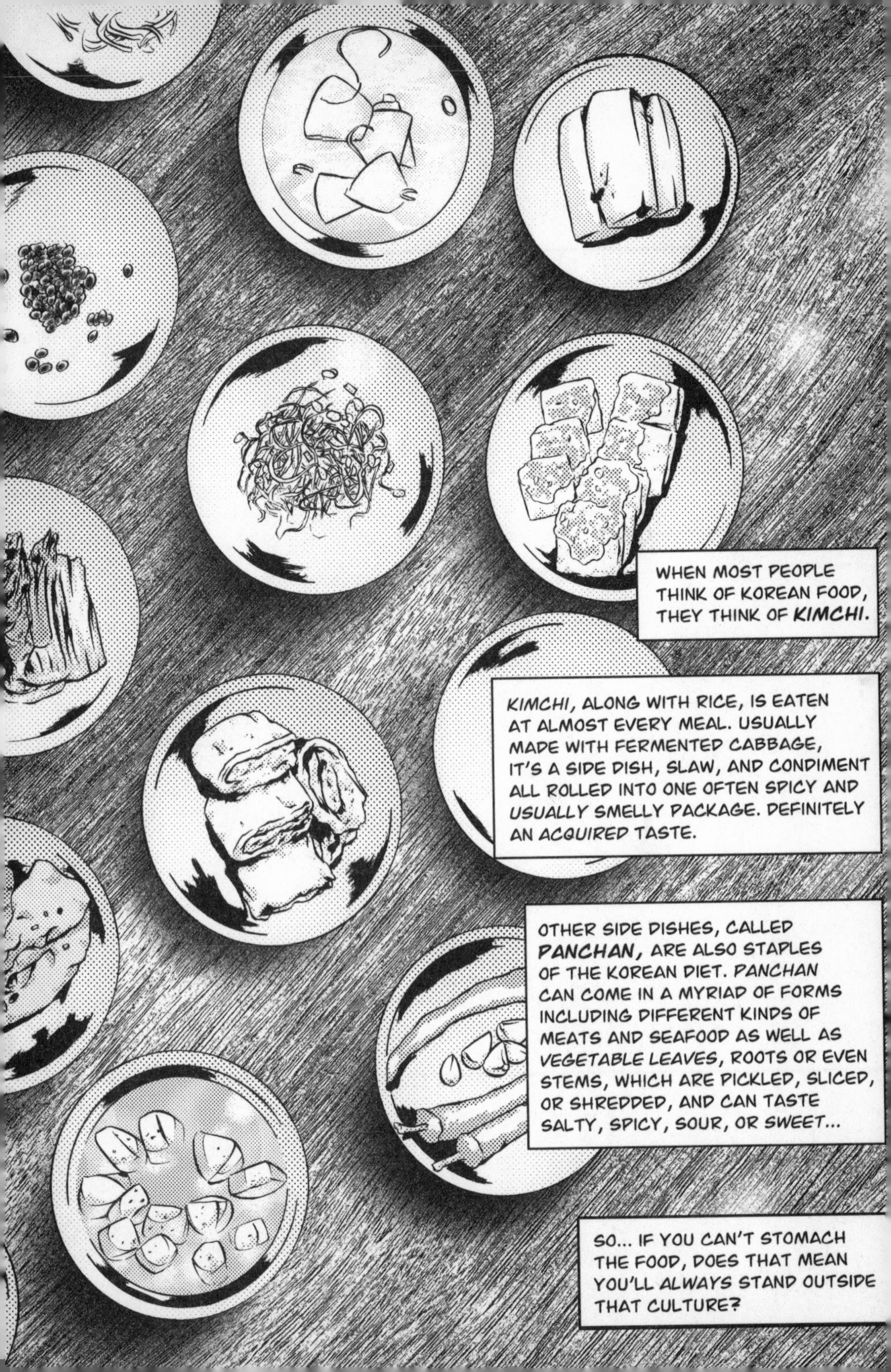
WHEN MOST PEOPLE THINK OF KOREAN FOOD, THEY THINK OF KIMCHI.
KIMCHI, ALONG WITH RICE, IS EATEN AT ALMOST EVERY MEAL. USUALLY MADE WITH FERMENTED CABBAGE, IT'S A SIDE DISH, SLAW, AND CONDIMENT ALL ROLLED INTO ONE OFTEN SPICY AND USUALLY SMELLY PACKAGE. DEFINITELY AN ACQUIRED TASTE.
OTHER SIDE DISHES, CALLED PANCHAN, ARE ALSO STAPLES OF THE KOREAN DIET. PANCHAN CAN COME IN A MYRIAD OF FORMS INCLUDING DIFFERENT KINDS OF MEATS AND SEAFOOD AS WELL AS VEGETABLE LEAVES, ROOTS OR EVEN STEMS, WHICH ARE PICKLED, SLICED, OR SHREDDED, AND CAN TASTE SALTY, SPICY, SOUR, OR SWEET...
SO... IF YOU CAN'T STOMACH THE FOOD, DOES THAT MEAN YOU'LL ALWAYS STAND OUTSIDE THAT CULTURE?

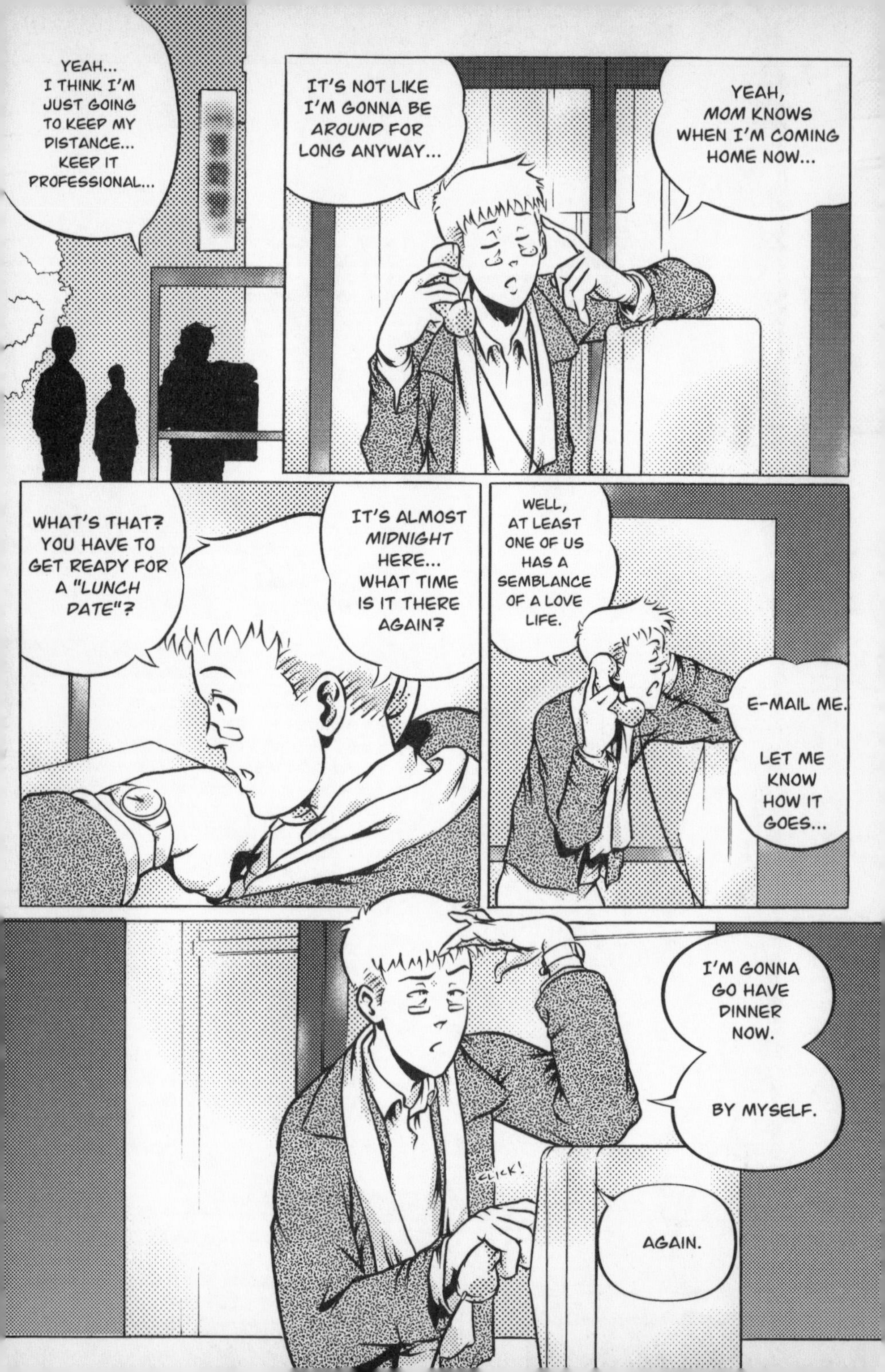
YEAH... I THINK I'M JUST GOING TO KEEP MY DISTANCE... KEEP IT PROFESSIONAL...
IT'S NOT LIKE I'M GONNA BE AROUND FOR LONG ANYWAY...
YEAH, MOM KNOWS WHEN I'M COMING HOME NOW...
WHAT'S THAT? YOU HAVE TO GET READY FOR A "LUNCH DATE"?
IT'S ALMOST MIDNIGHT HERE... WHAT TIME IS IT THERE AGAIN?
WELL, AT LEAST ONE OF US HAS A SEMBLANCE OF A LOVE LIFE.
E-MAIL ME.
LET ME KNOW HOW IT GOES...
I'M GONNA GO HAVE DINNER NOW.
BY MYSELF.
CLICK!
AGAIN.

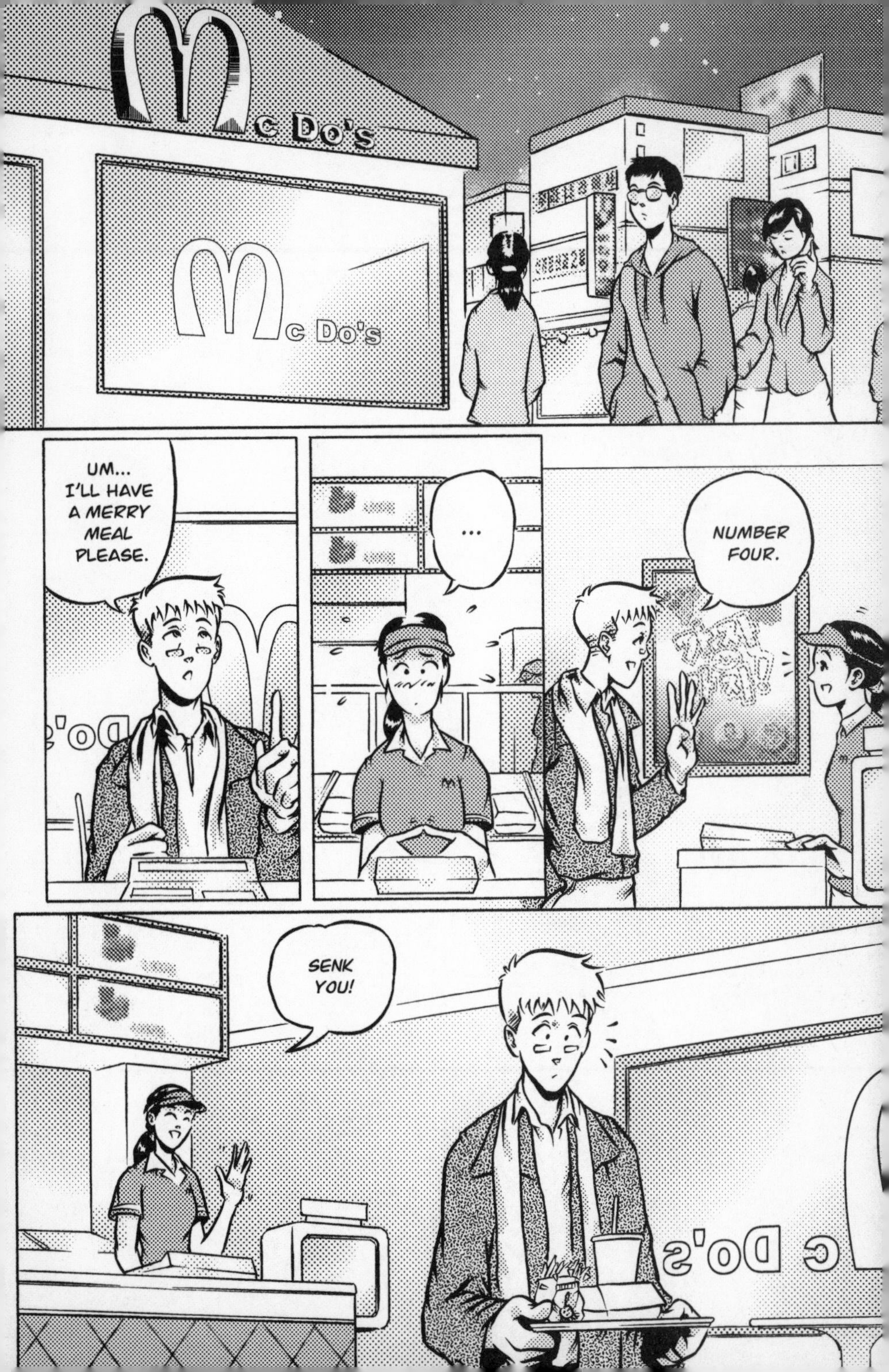
Mc Do's
Mc Do's
UM... I'LL HAVE A MERRY MEAL PLEASE.
...
NUMBER FOUR.
SENK YOU!

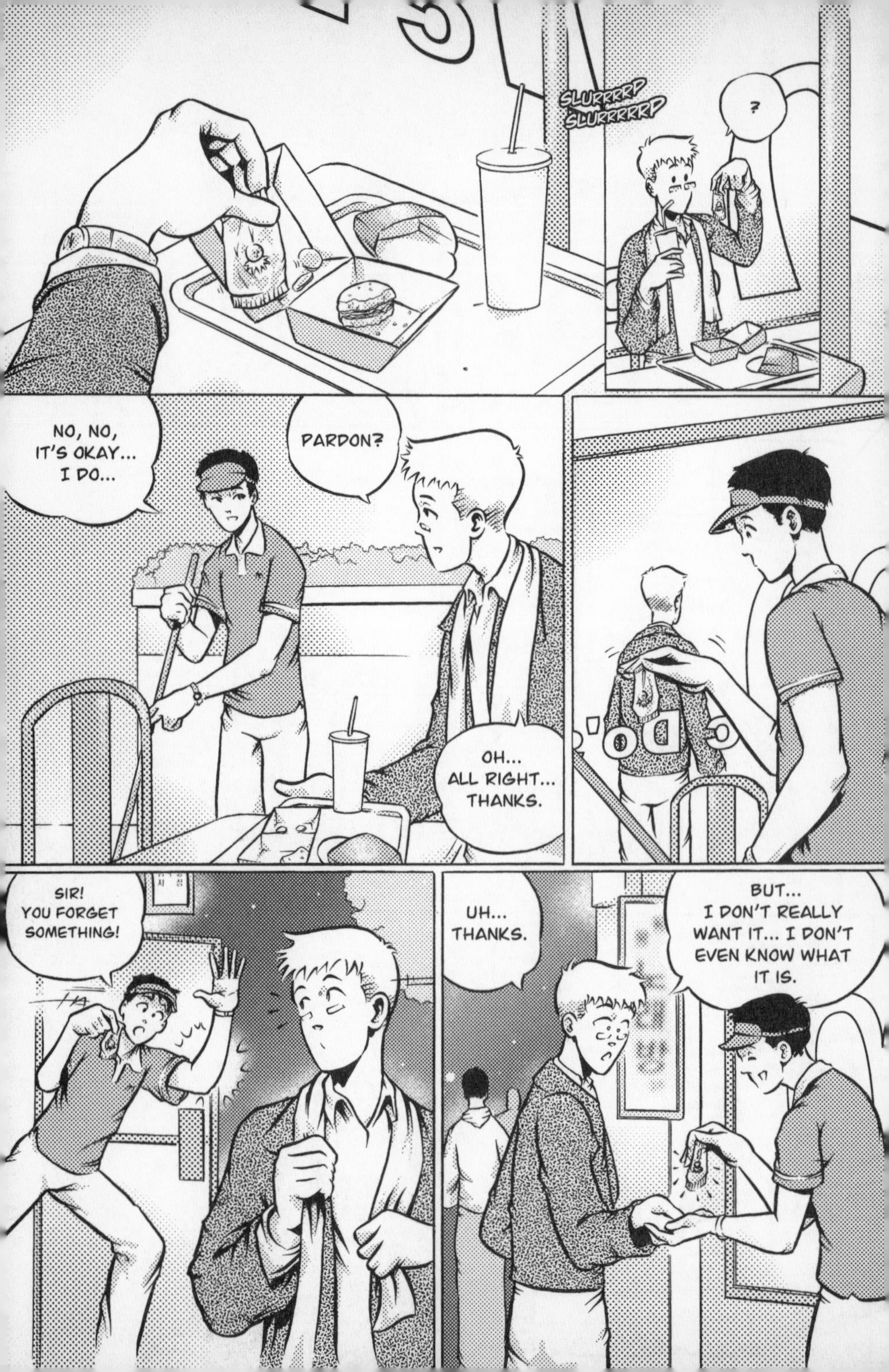

SLURRRRP
SLURRRRRP
?
NO, NO, IT'S OKAY... I DO...
PARDON?
OH... ALL RIGHT... THANKS.
SIR! YOU FORGET SOMETHING!
UH... THANKS.
BUT... I DON'T REALLY WANT IT... I DON'T EVEN KNOW WHAT IT IS.

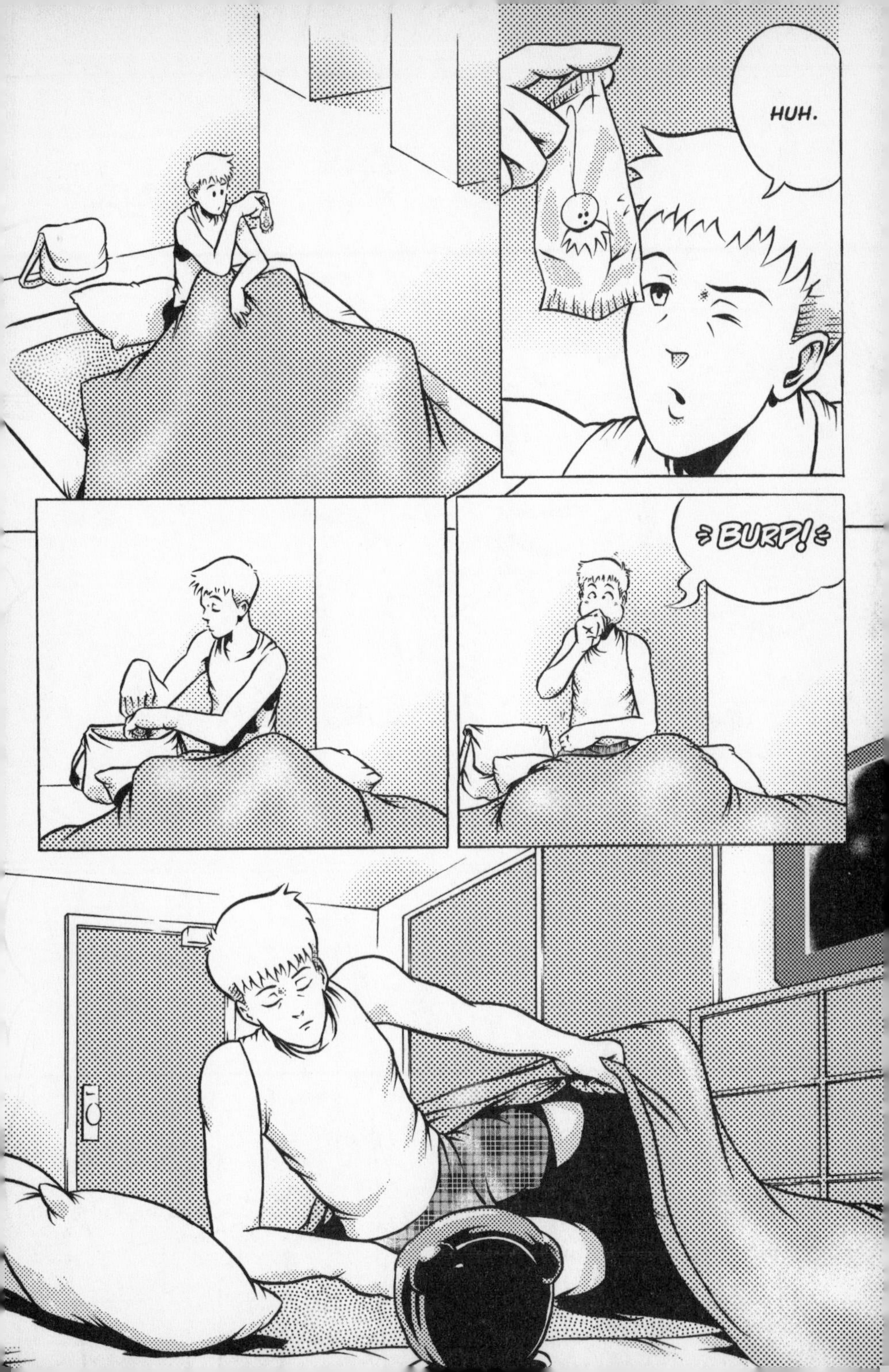
HUH.
BURP!

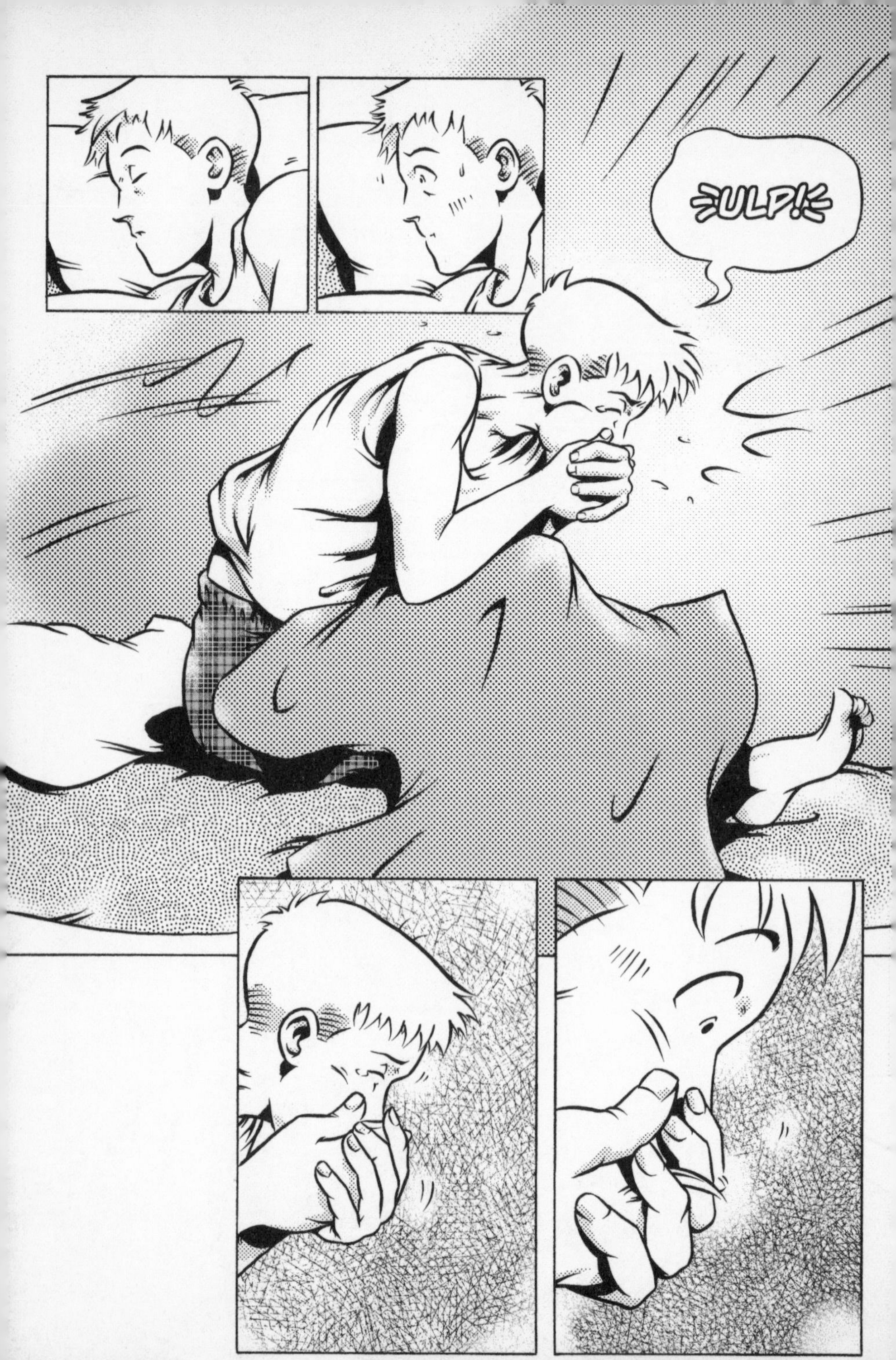
ULP!

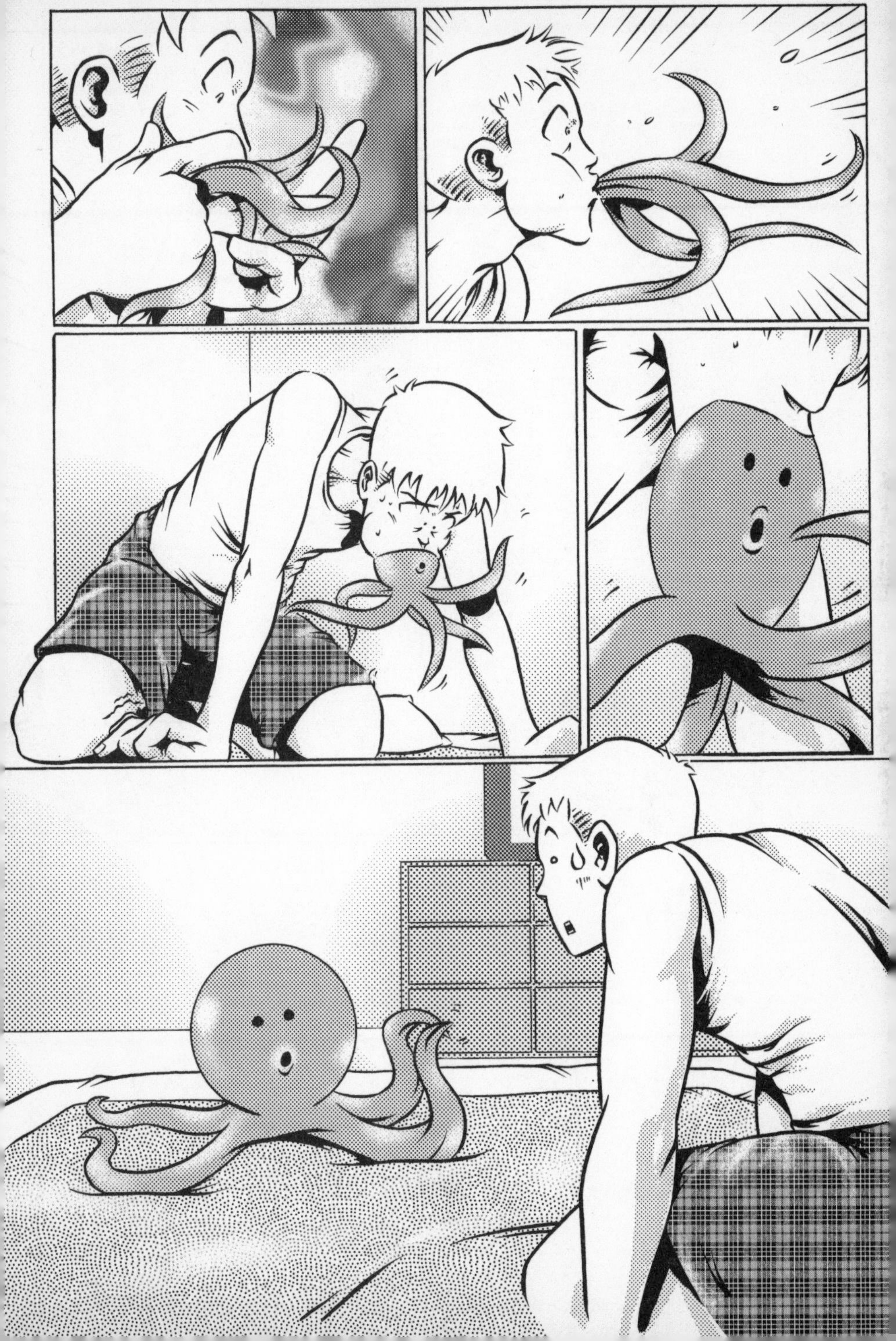

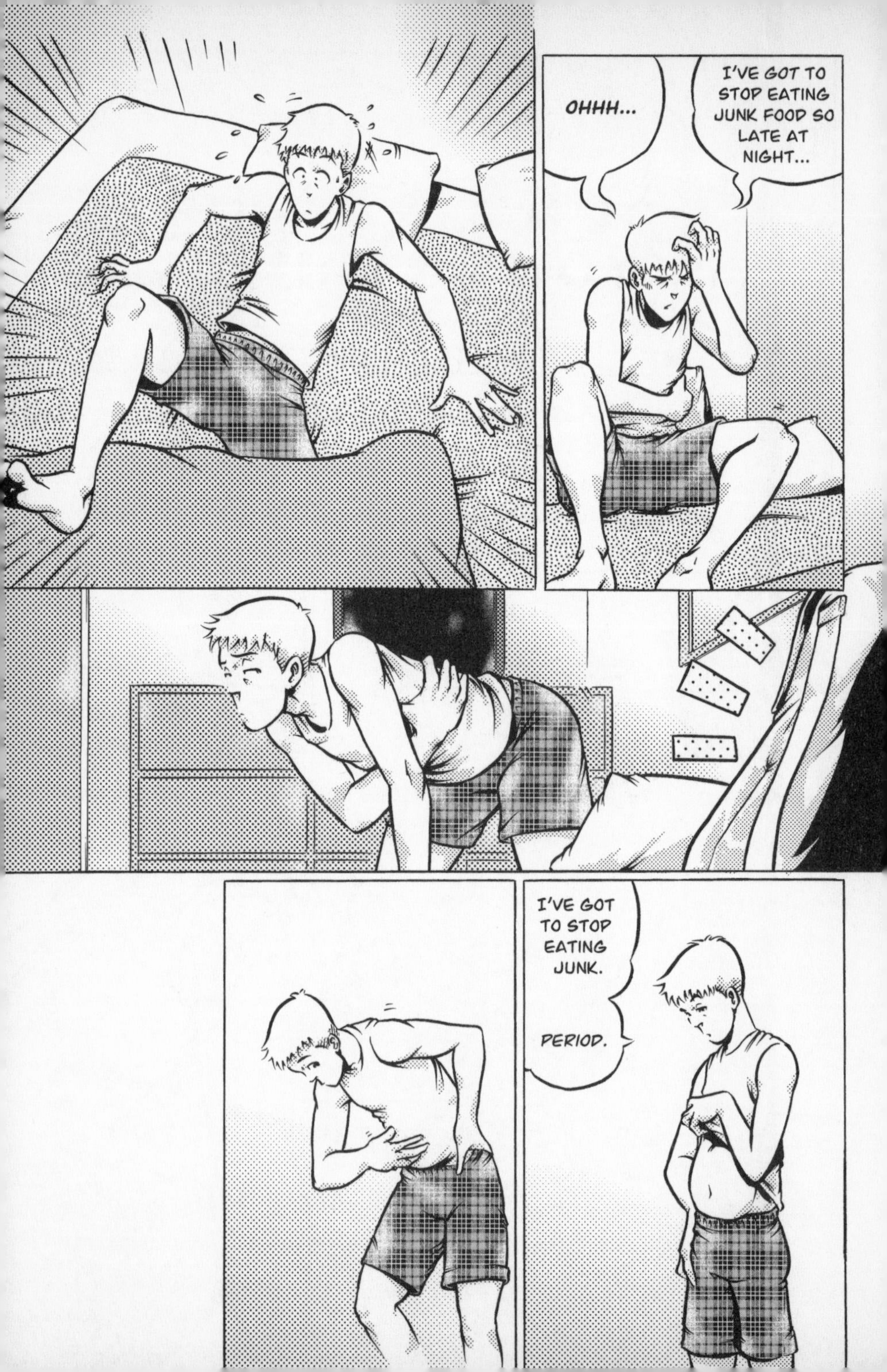
OHHH...
I'VE GOT TO STOP EATING JUNK FOOD SO LATE AT NIGHT...
I'VE GOT TO STOP EATING JUNK.
PERIOD.

Chapter 10

DON'T NAK-JI TIL YOU'VE TRIED JI

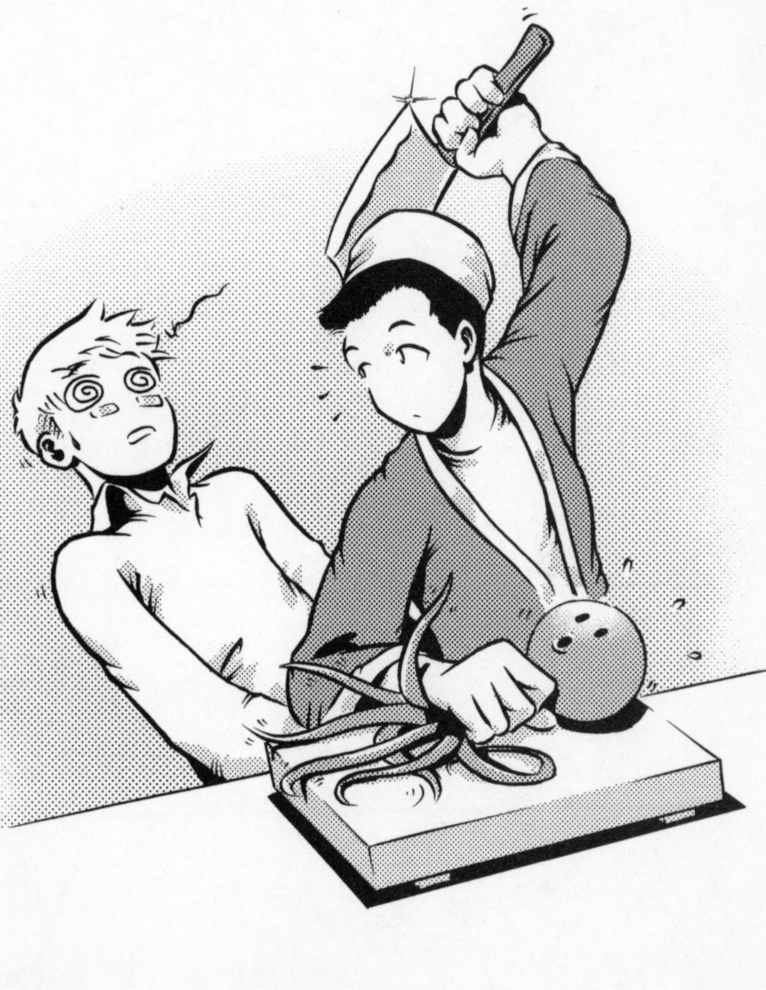

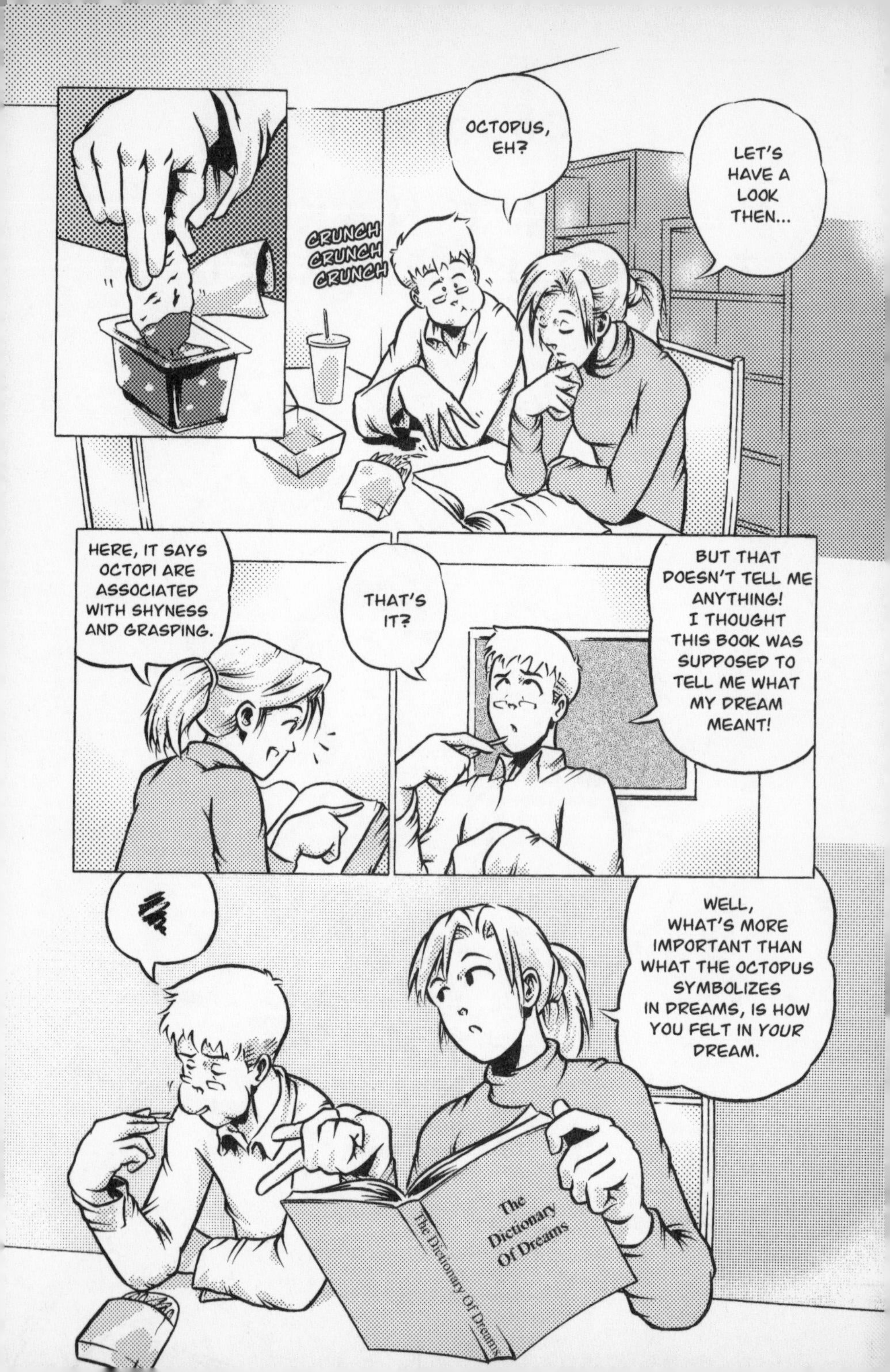
CRUNCH CRUNCH CRUNCH
OCTOPUS, EH?
LET'S HAVE A LOOK THEN...
HERE, IT SAYS OCTOPI ARE ASSOCIATED WITH SHYNESS AND GRASPING.
THAT'S IT?
BUT THAT DOESN'T TELL ME ANYTHING! I THOUGHT THIS BOOK WAS SUPPOSED TO TELL ME WHAT MY DREAM MEANT!
WELL, WHAT'S MORE IMPORTANT THAN WHAT THE OCTOPUS SYMBOLIZES IN DREAMS, IS HOW YOU FELT IN *YOUR* DREAM.
The Dictionary Of Dreams
The Dictionary Of Dreams

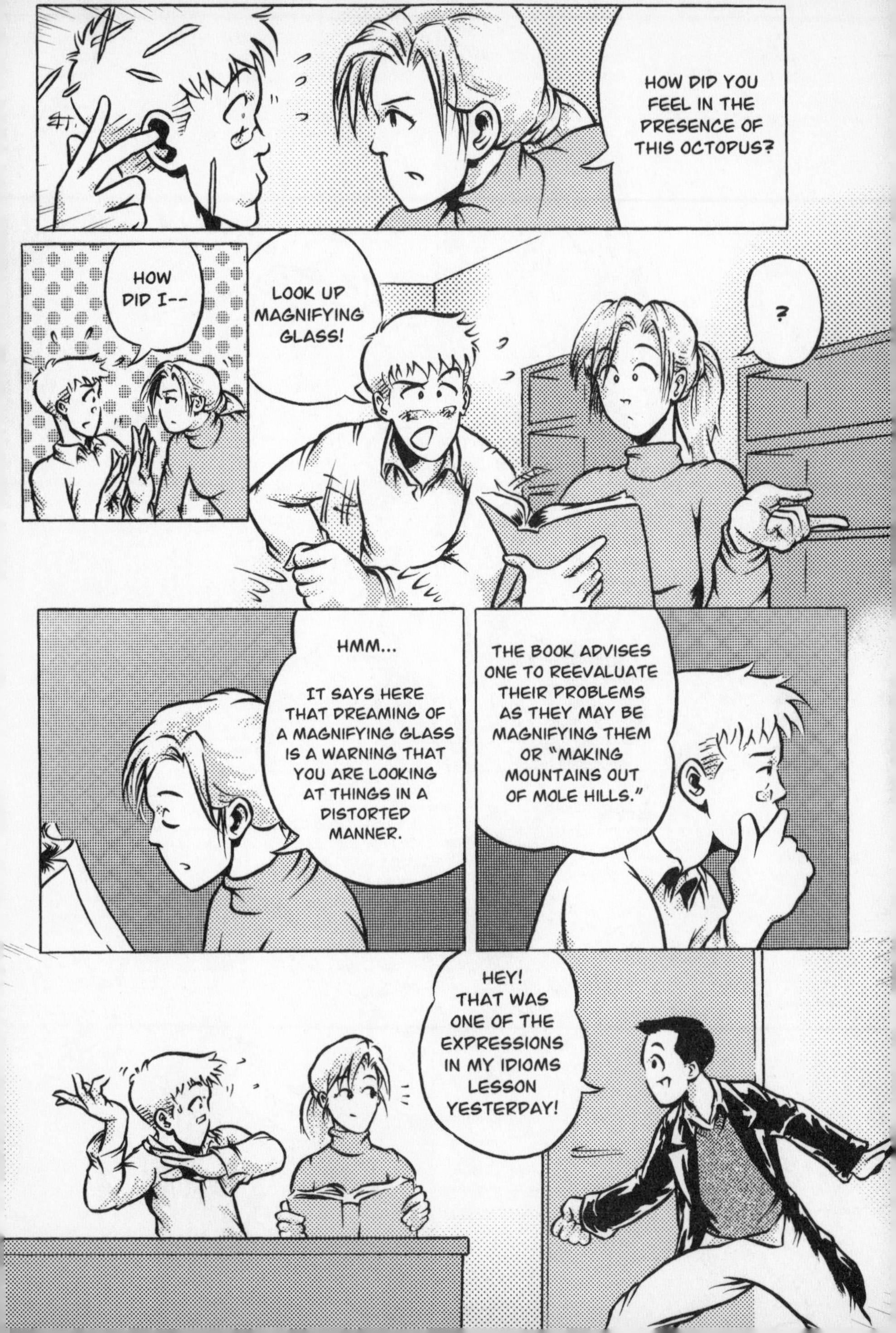
HOW DID YOU FEEL IN THE PRESENCE OF THIS OCTOPUS?
HOW DID I--
LOOK UP MAGNIFYING GLASS!
?
HMM...
IT SAYS HERE THAT DREAMING OF A MAGNIFYING GLASS IS A WARNING THAT YOU ARE LOOKING AT THINGS IN A DISTORTED MANNER.
THE BOOK ADVISES ONE TO REEVALUATE THEIR PROBLEMS AS THEY MAY BE MAGNIFYING THEM OR "MAKING MOUNTAINS OUT OF MOLE HILLS."
HEY! THAT WAS ONE OF THE EXPRESSIONS IN MY IDIOMS LESSON YESTERDAY!

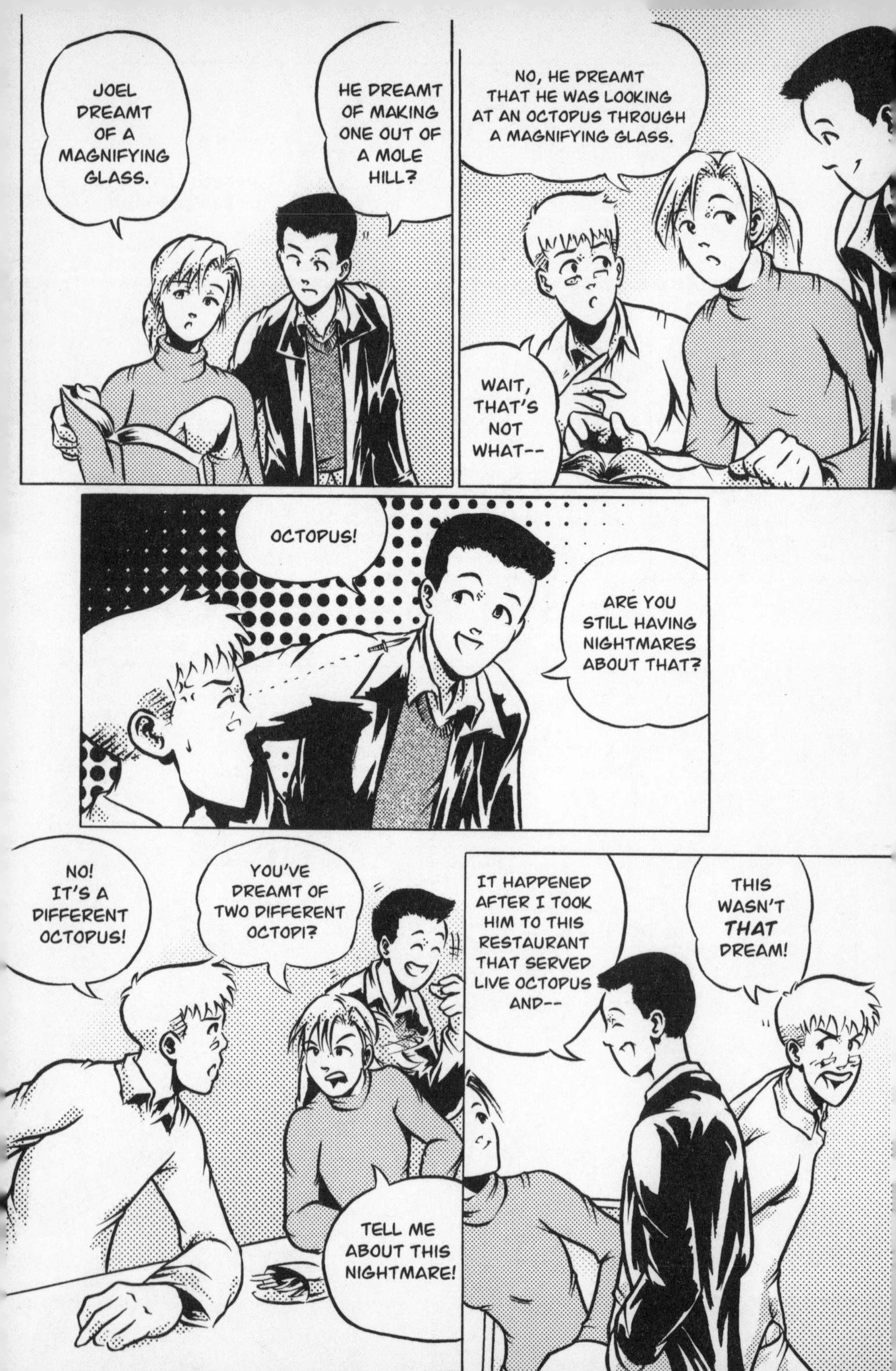
JOEL DREAMT OF A MAGNIFYING GLASS.
HE DREAMT OF MAKING ONE OUT OF A MOLE HILL?
NO, HE DREAMT THAT HE WAS LOOKING AT AN OCTOPUS THROUGH A MAGNIFYING GLASS.
WAIT, THAT'S NOT WHAT--
OCTOPUS!
ARE YOU STILL HAVING NIGHTMARES ABOUT THAT?
NO! IT'S A DIFFERENT OCTOPUS!
YOU'VE DREAMT OF TWO DIFFERENT OCTOPI?
TELL ME ABOUT THIS NIGHTMARE!
IT HAPPENED AFTER I TOOK HIM TO THIS RESTAURANT THAT SERVED LIVE OCTOPUS AND--
THIS WASN'T THAT DREAM!

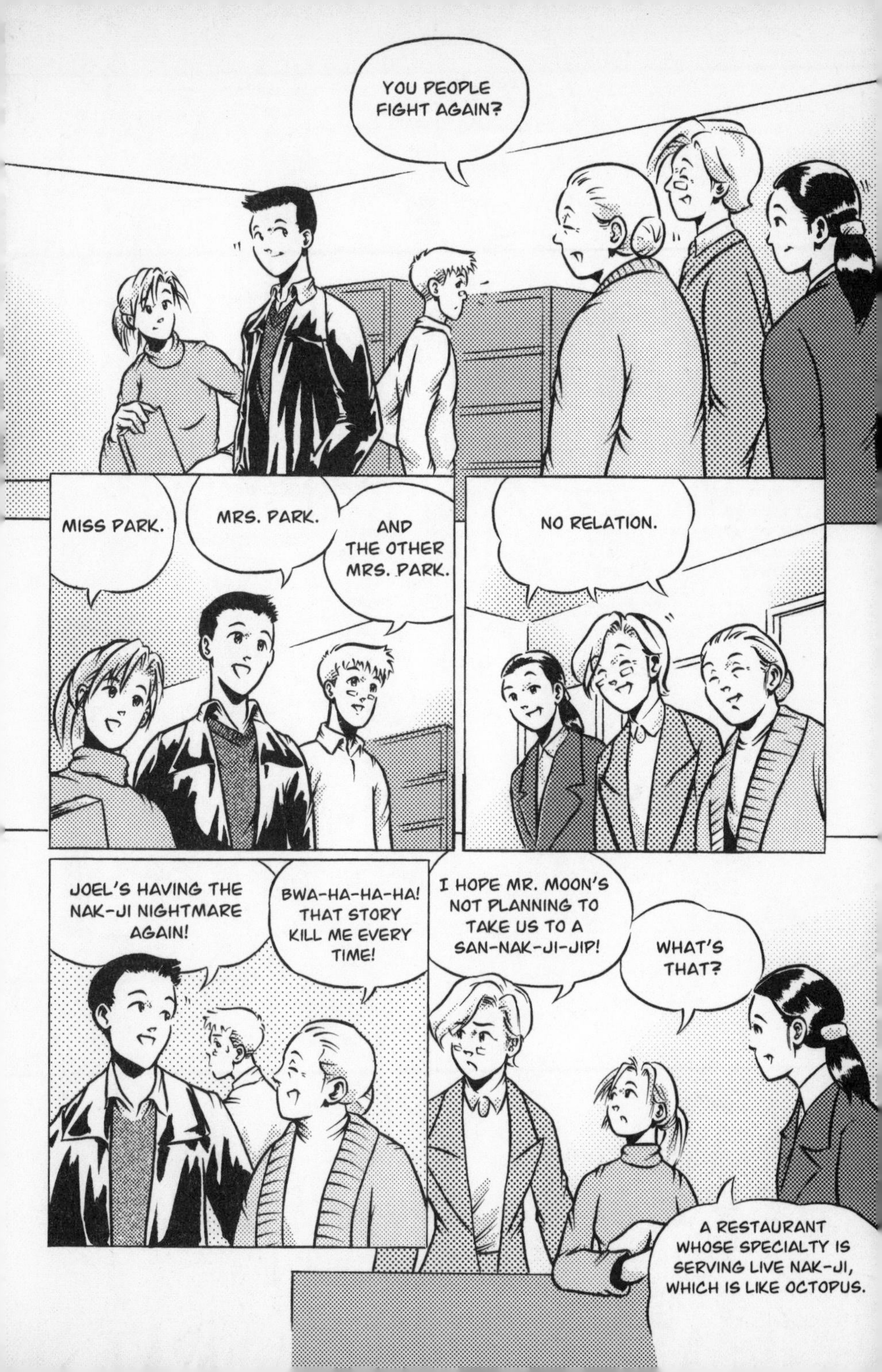
YOU PEOPLE FIGHT AGAIN?
MISS PARK.
MRS. PARK.
AND THE OTHER MRS. PARK.
NO RELATION.
JOEL'S HAVING THE NAK-JI NIGHTMARE AGAIN!
BWA-HA-HA-HA! THAT STORY KILL ME EVERY TIME!
I HOPE MR. MOON'S NOT PLANNING TO TAKE US TO A SAN-NAK-JI-JIP!
WHAT'S THAT?
A RESTAURANT WHOSE SPECIALTY IS SERVING LIVE NAK-JI, WHICH IS LIKE OCTOPUS.

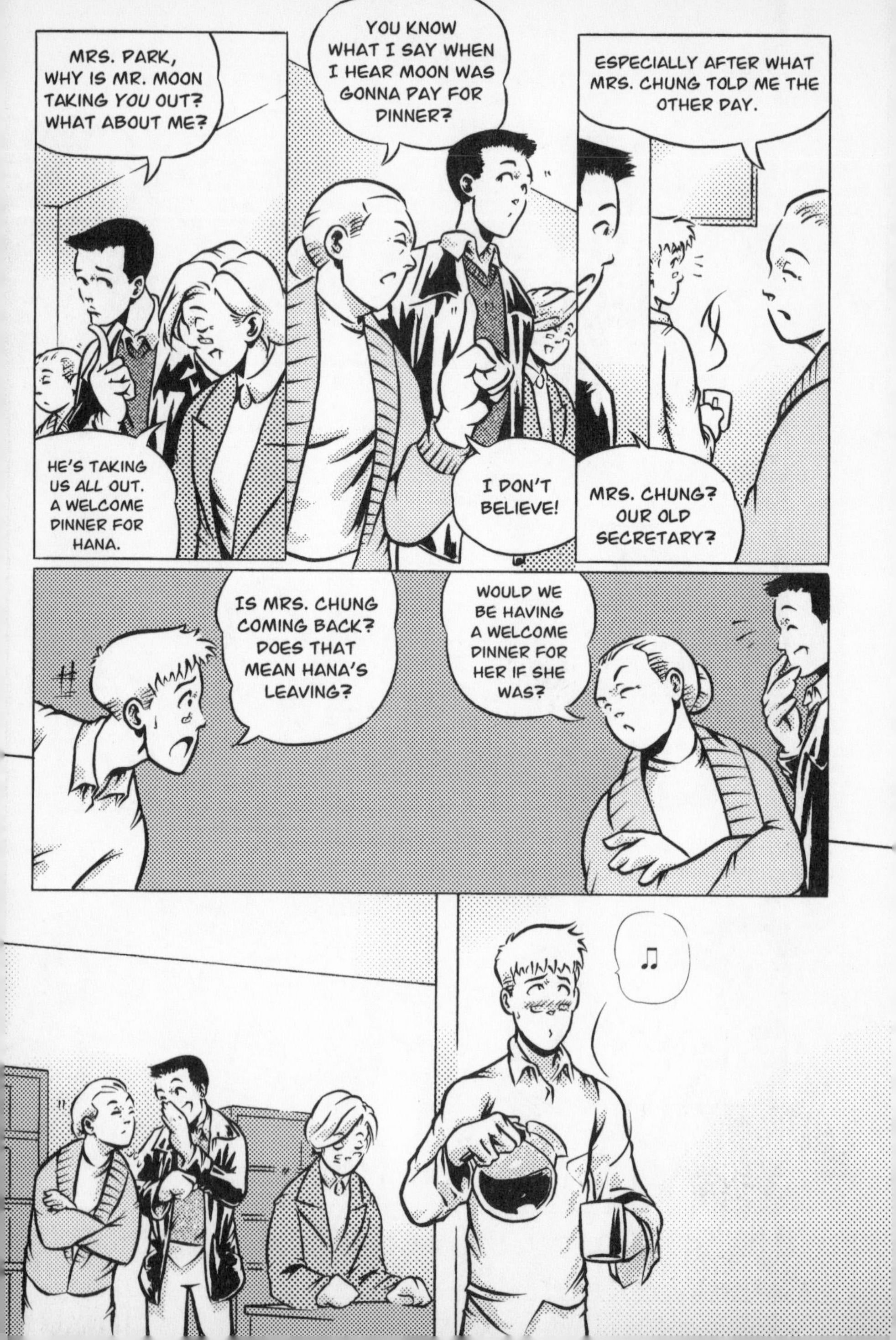
MRS. PARK, WHY IS MR. MOON TAKING YOU OUT? WHAT ABOUT ME?
YOU KNOW WHAT I SAY WHEN I HEAR MOON WAS GONNA PAY FOR DINNER?
ESPECIALLY AFTER WHAT MRS. CHUNG TOLD ME THE OTHER DAY.
HE'S TAKING US ALL OUT. A WELCOME DINNER FOR HANA.
I DON'T BELIEVE!
MRS. CHUNG? OUR OLD SECRETARY?
IS MRS. CHUNG COMING BACK? DOES THAT MEAN HANA'S LEAVING?
WOULD WE BE HAVING A WELCOME DINNER FOR HER IF SHE WAS?
♫

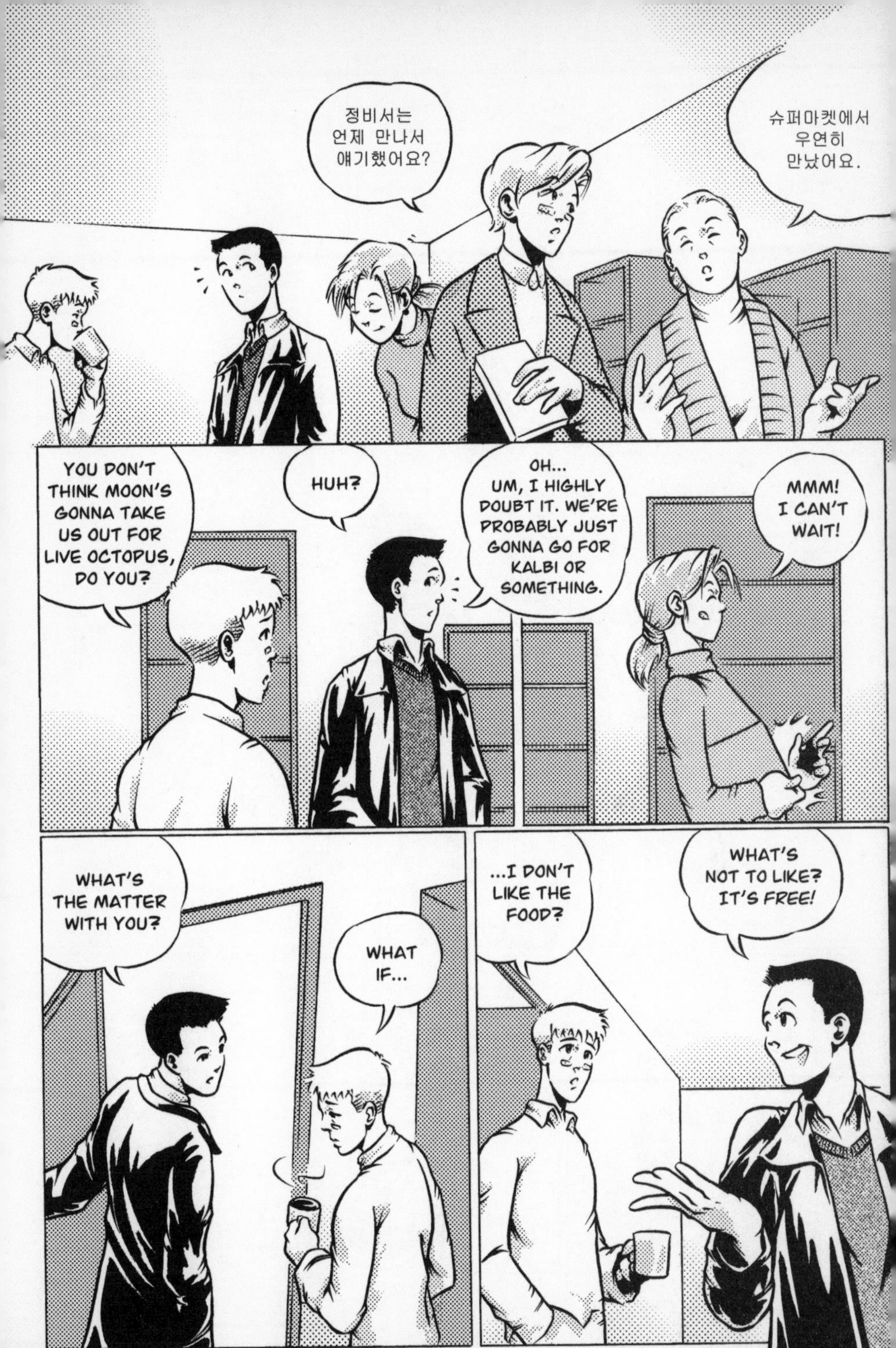
정비서는
언제 만나서
얘기했어요?
슈퍼마켓에서
우연히
만났어요.
YOU DON'T THINK MOON'S GONNA TAKE US OUT FOR LIVE OCTOPUS, DO YOU?
HUH?
OH... UM, I HIGHLY DOUBT IT. WE'RE PROBABLY JUST GONNA GO FOR KALBI OR SOMETHING.
MMM! I CAN'T WAIT!
WHAT'S THE MATTER WITH YOU?
WHAT IF...
...I DON'T LIKE THE FOOD?
WHAT'S NOT TO LIKE? IT'S FREE!

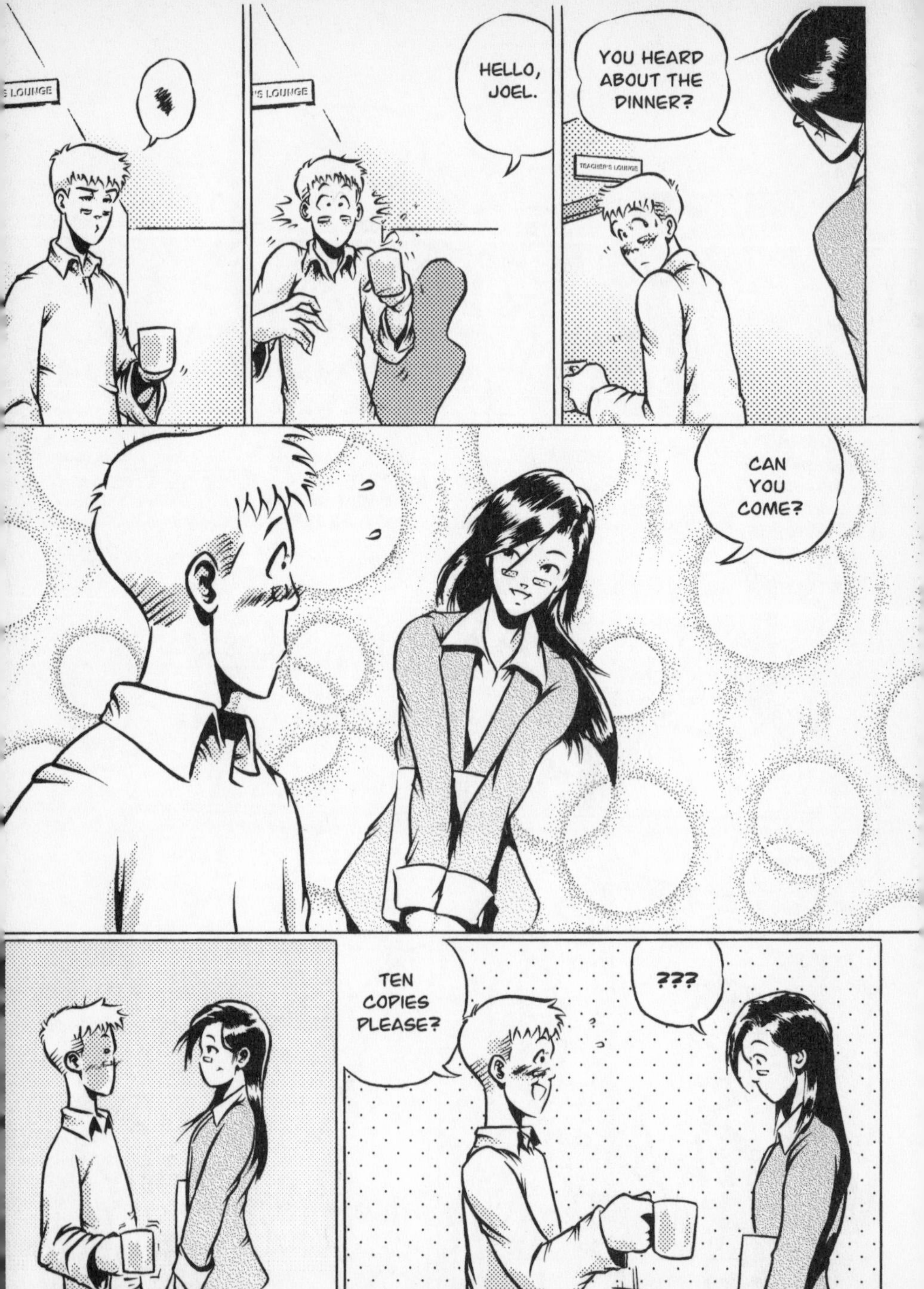
'S LOUNGE
'S LOUNGE
HELLO, JOEL.
TEACHER'S LOUNGE
YOU HEARD ABOUT THE DINNER?
CAN YOU COME?
TEN COPIES PLEASE?
???

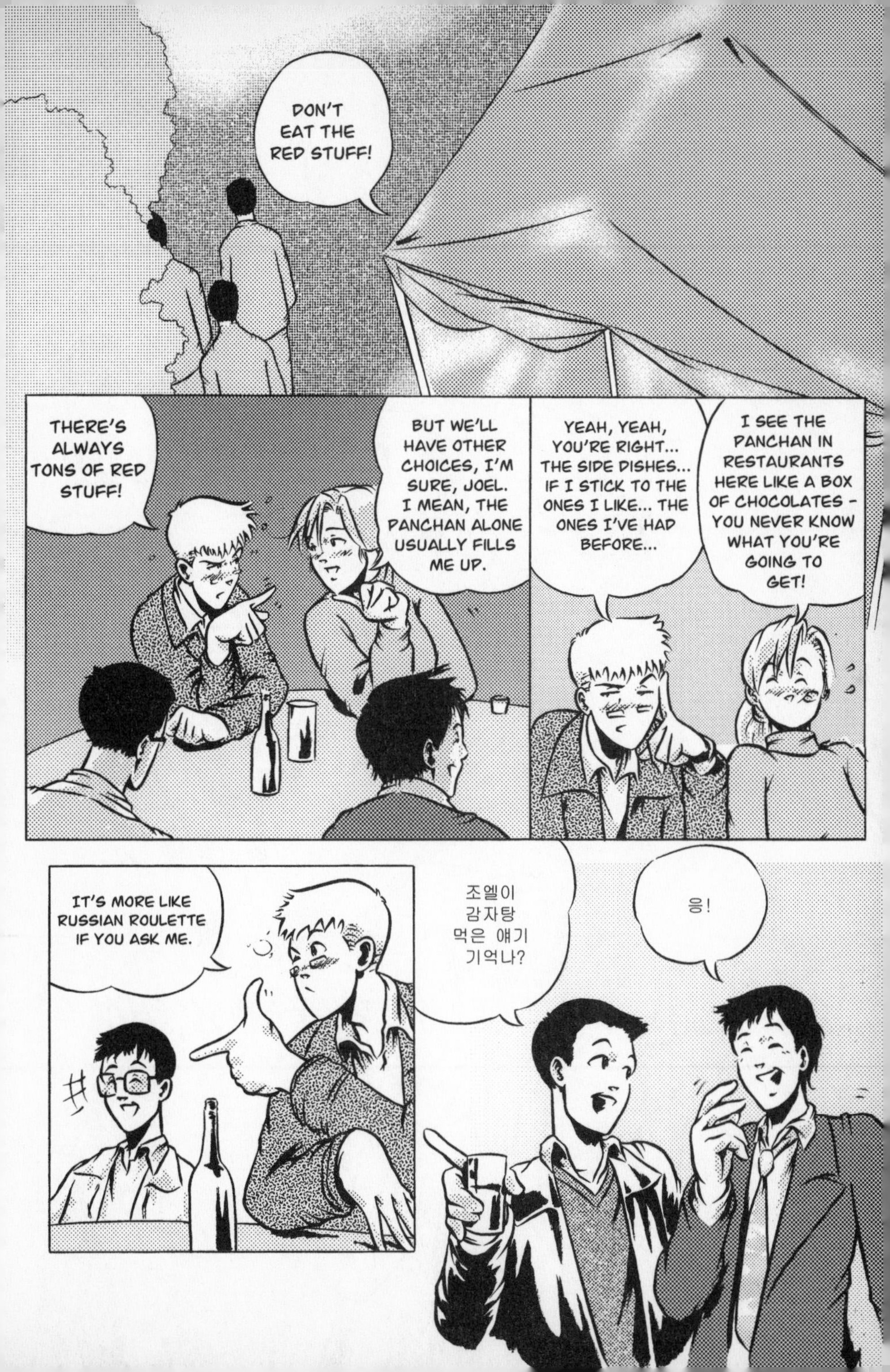
DON'T EAT THE RED STUFF!
THERE'S ALWAYS TONS OF RED STUFF!
BUT WE'LL HAVE OTHER CHOICES, I'M SURE, JOEL. I MEAN, THE PANCHAN ALONE USUALLY FILLS ME UP.
YEAH, YEAH, YOU'RE RIGHT... THE SIDE DISHES... IF I STICK TO THE ONES I LIKE... THE ONES I'VE HAD BEFORE...
I SEE THE PANCHAN IN RESTAURANTS HERE LIKE A BOX OF CHOCOLATES - YOU NEVER KNOW WHAT YOU'RE GOING TO GET!
IT'S MORE LIKE RUSSIAN ROULETTE IF YOU ASK ME.
조엘이 감자탕 먹은 얘기 기억나?
응!

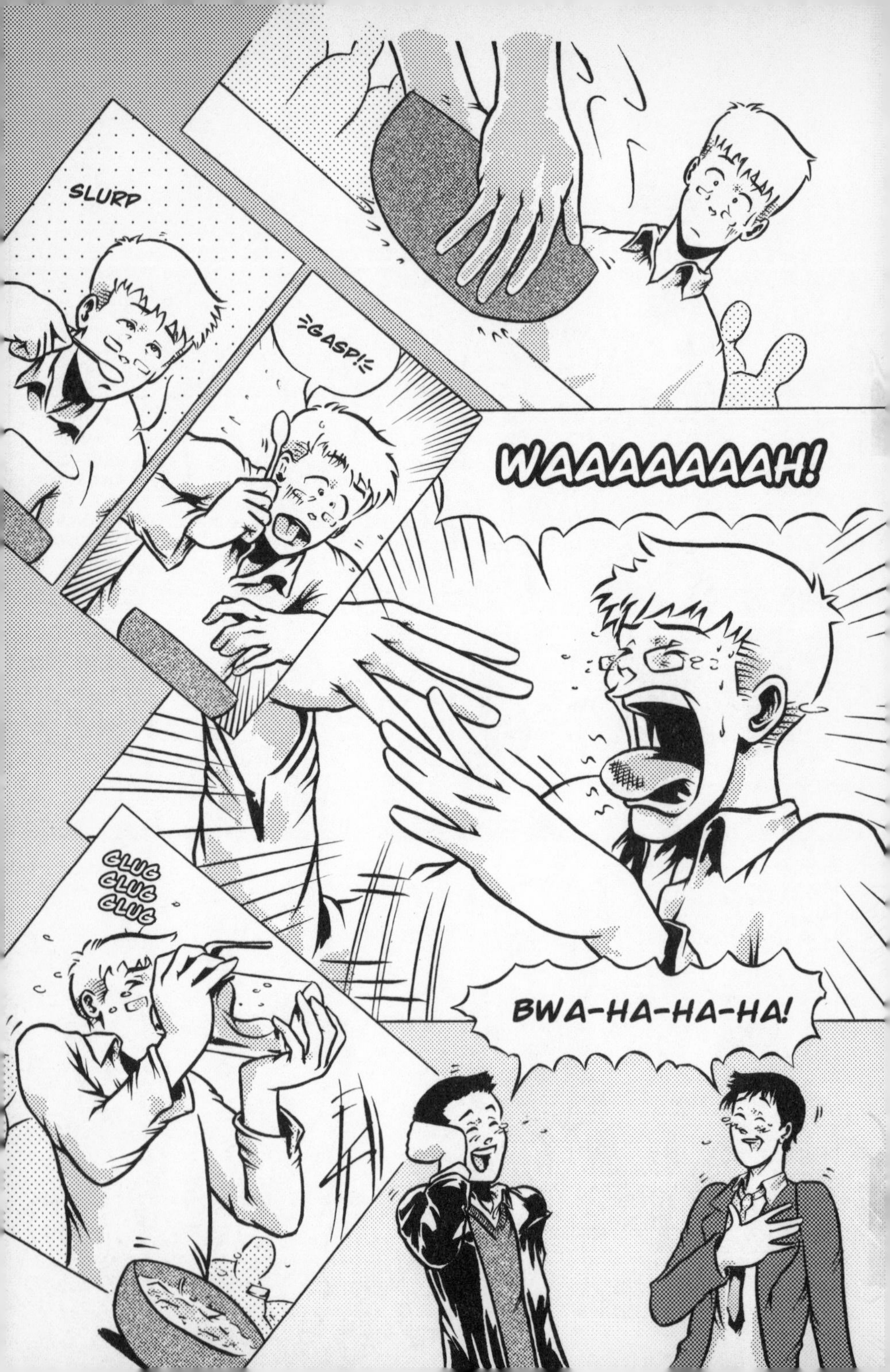
SLURP
GASP!
WAAAAAAAAH!
GLUG
GLUG
GLUG
BWA-HA-HA-HA!

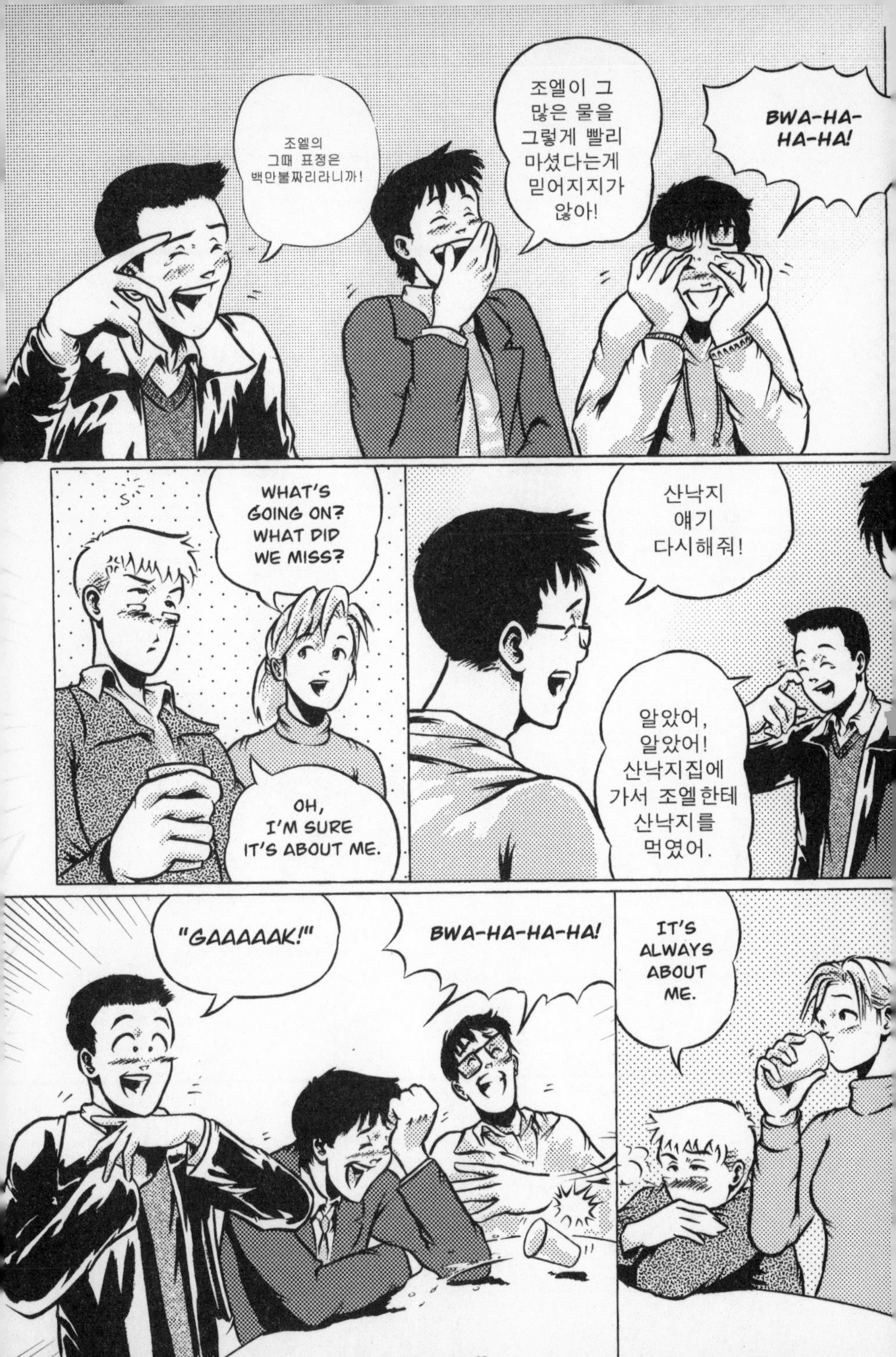
조엘의
그때 표정은
백만불짜리라니까!
조엘이 그
많은 물을
그렇게 빨리
마셨다는게
믿어지지가
않아!
BWA-HA-
HA-HA!
WHAT'S
GOING ON?
WHAT DID
WE MISS?
OH,
I'M SURE
IT'S ABOUT ME.
산낙지
얘기
다시해줘!
알았어,
알았어!
산낙지집에
가서 조엘한테
산낙지를
먹였어.
"GAAAAAK!"
BWA-HA-HA-HA!
IT'S
ALWAYS
ABOUT
ME.

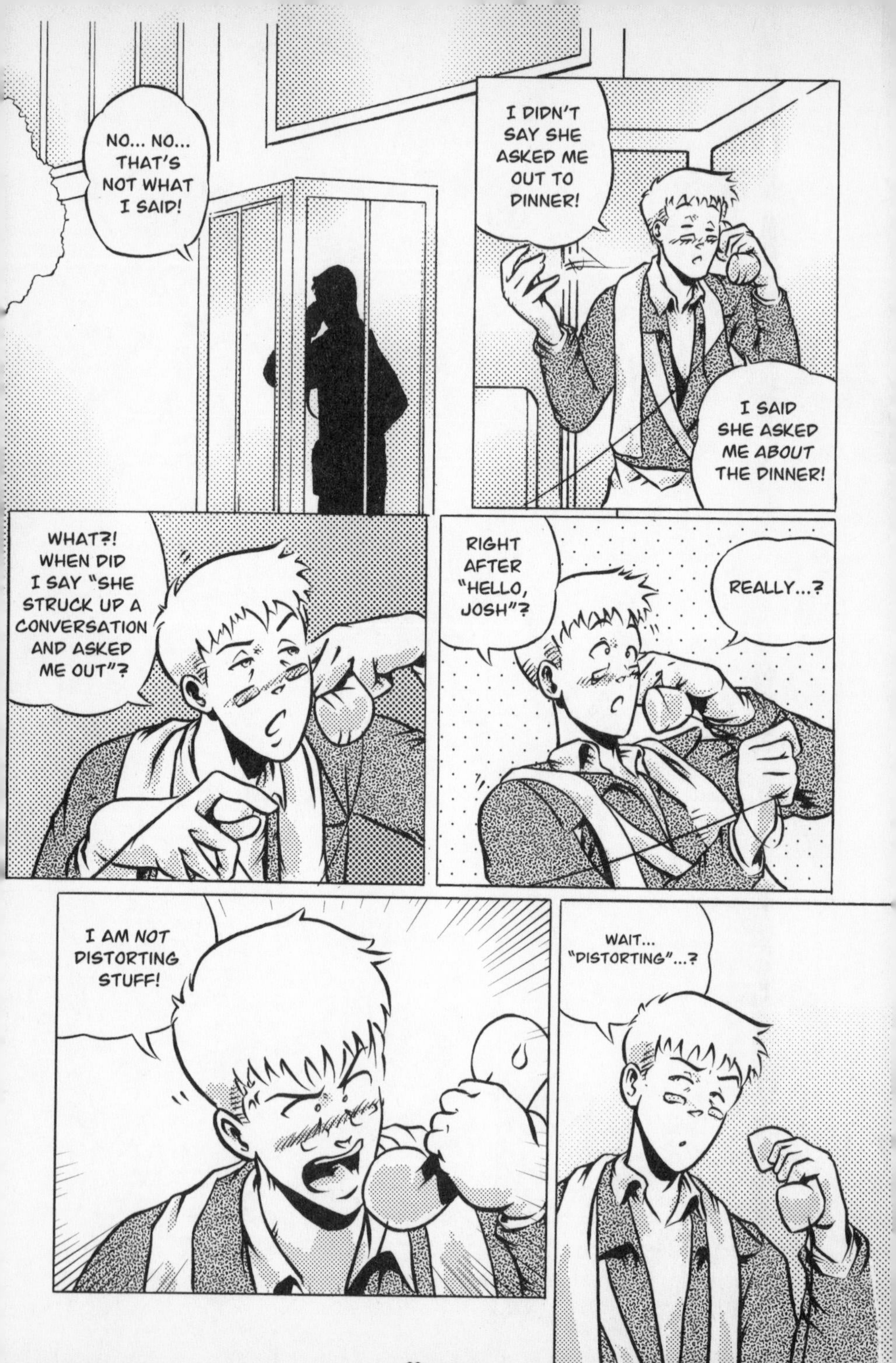
NO... NO... THAT'S NOT WHAT I SAID!
I DIDN'T SAY SHE ASKED ME OUT TO DINNER!
I SAID SHE ASKED ME ABOUT THE DINNER!
WHAT?! WHEN DID I SAY "SHE STRUCK UP A CONVERSATION AND ASKED ME OUT"?
RIGHT AFTER "HELLO, JOSH"?
REALLY...?
I AM NOT DISTORTING STUFF!
WAIT... "DISTORTING"...?

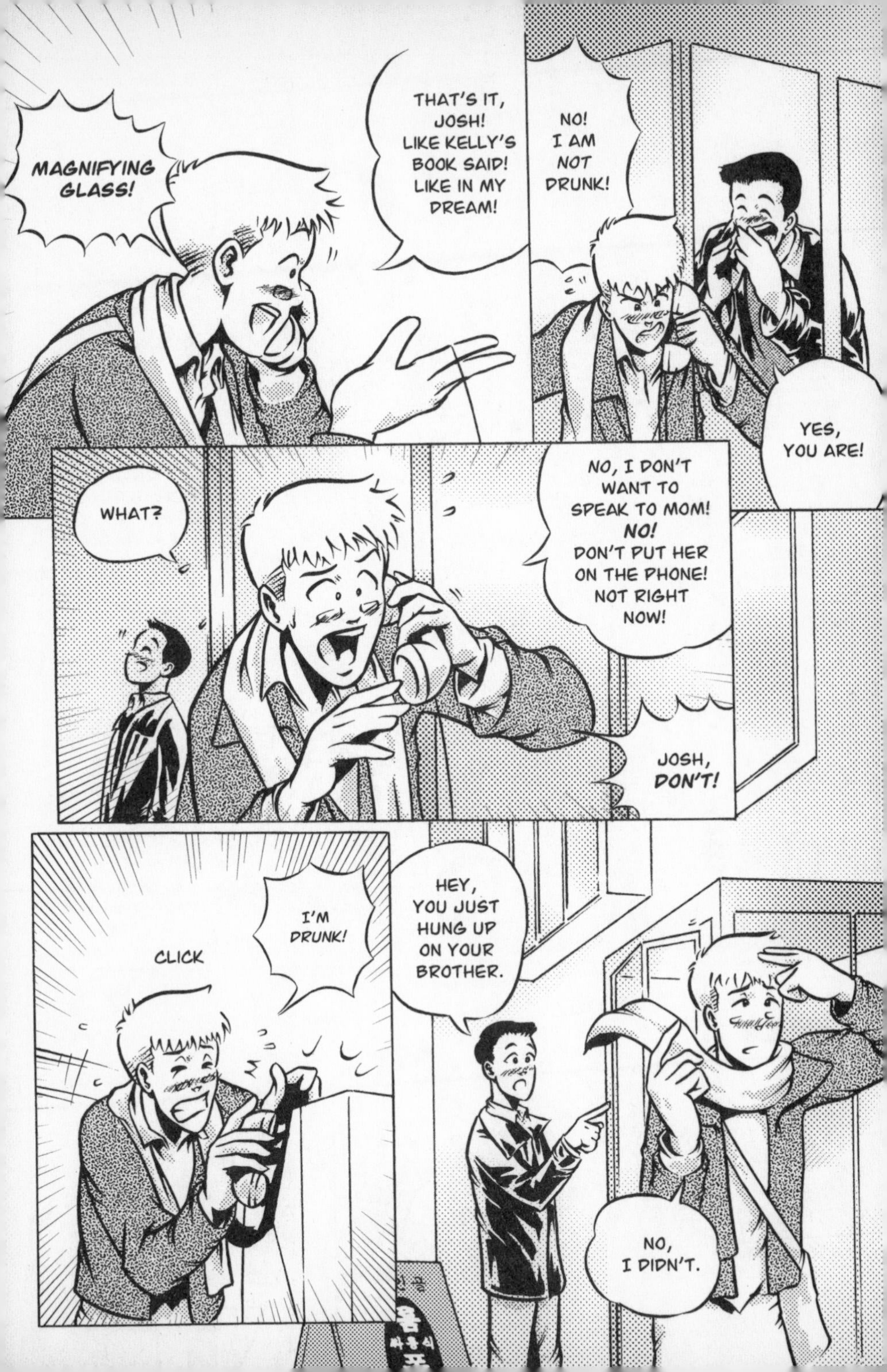
MAGNIFYING GLASS!
THAT'S IT, JOSH! LIKE KELLY'S BOOK SAID! LIKE IN MY DREAM!
NO! I AM NOT DRUNK!
YES, YOU ARE!
WHAT?
NO, I DON'T WANT TO SPEAK TO MOM! NO! DON'T PUT HER ON THE PHONE! NOT RIGHT NOW!
JOSH, DON'T!
CLICK
I'M DRUNK!
HEY, YOU JUST HUNG UP ON YOUR BROTHER.
NO, I DIDN'T.

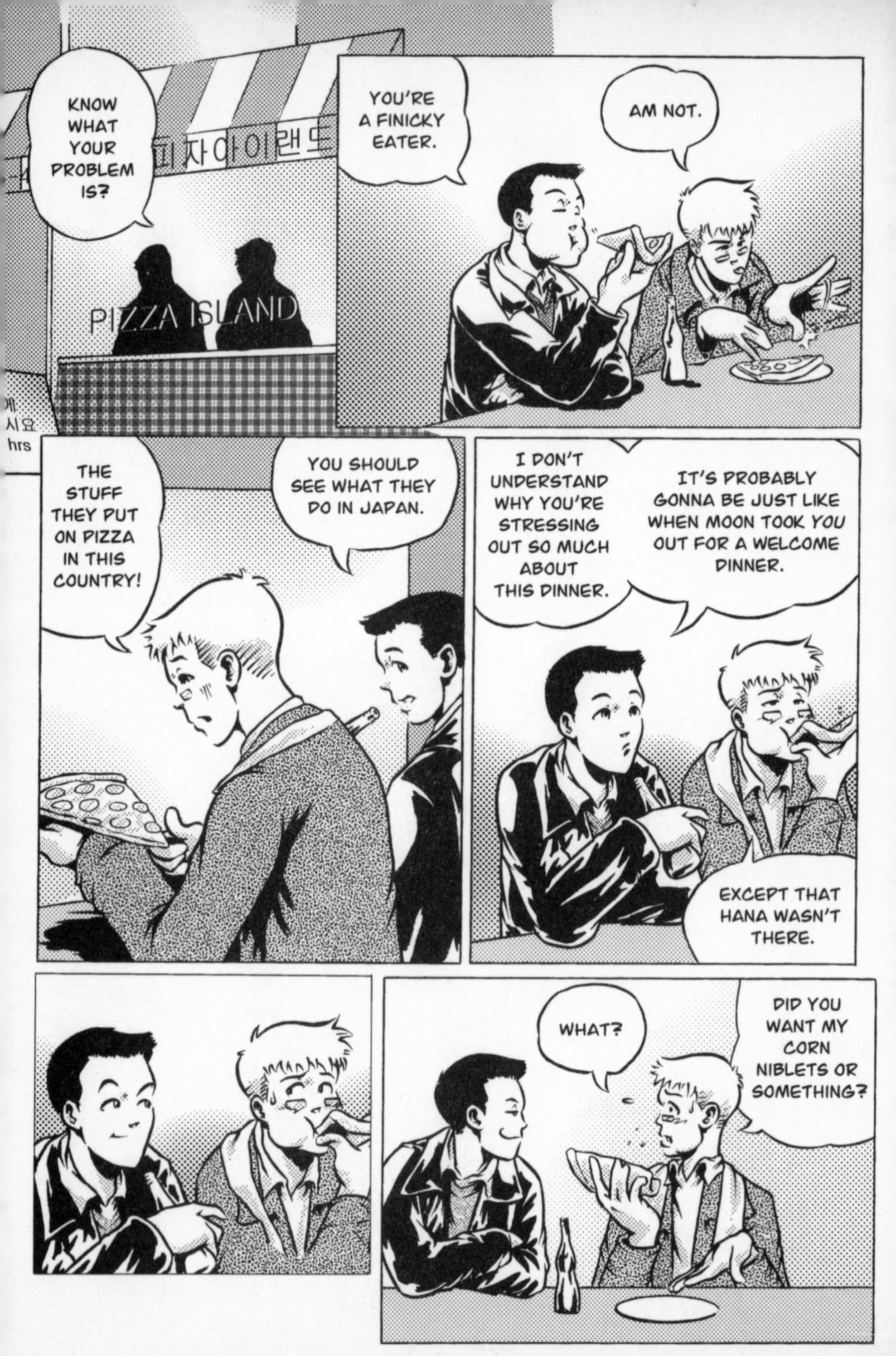
KNOW WHAT YOUR PROBLEM IS?
PIZZA ISLAND
YOU'RE A FINICKY EATER.
AM NOT.
THE STUFF THEY PUT ON PIZZA IN THIS COUNTRY!
YOU SHOULD SEE WHAT THEY DO IN JAPAN.
I DON'T UNDERSTAND WHY YOU'RE STRESSING OUT SO MUCH ABOUT THIS DINNER.
IT'S PROBABLY GONNA BE JUST LIKE WHEN MOON TOOK *YOU* OUT FOR A WELCOME DINNER.
EXCEPT THAT HANA WASN'T THERE.
WHAT?
DID YOU WANT MY CORN NIBLETS OR SOMETHING?

Chapter 11

CHEK YOUR HEAD

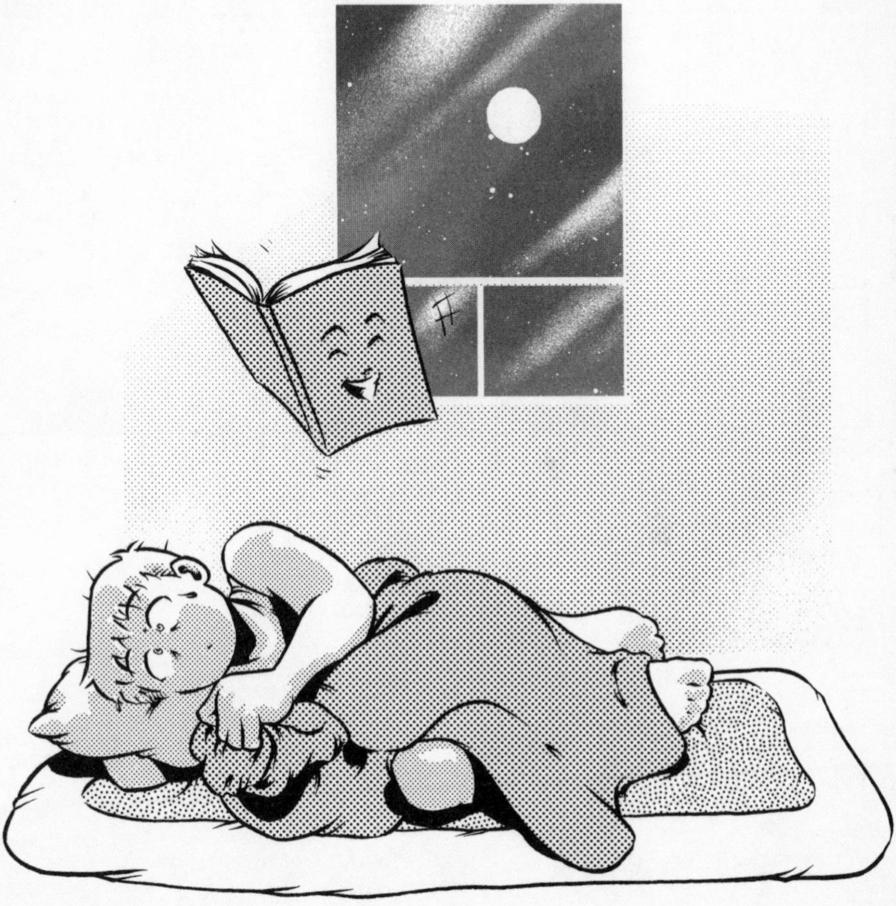

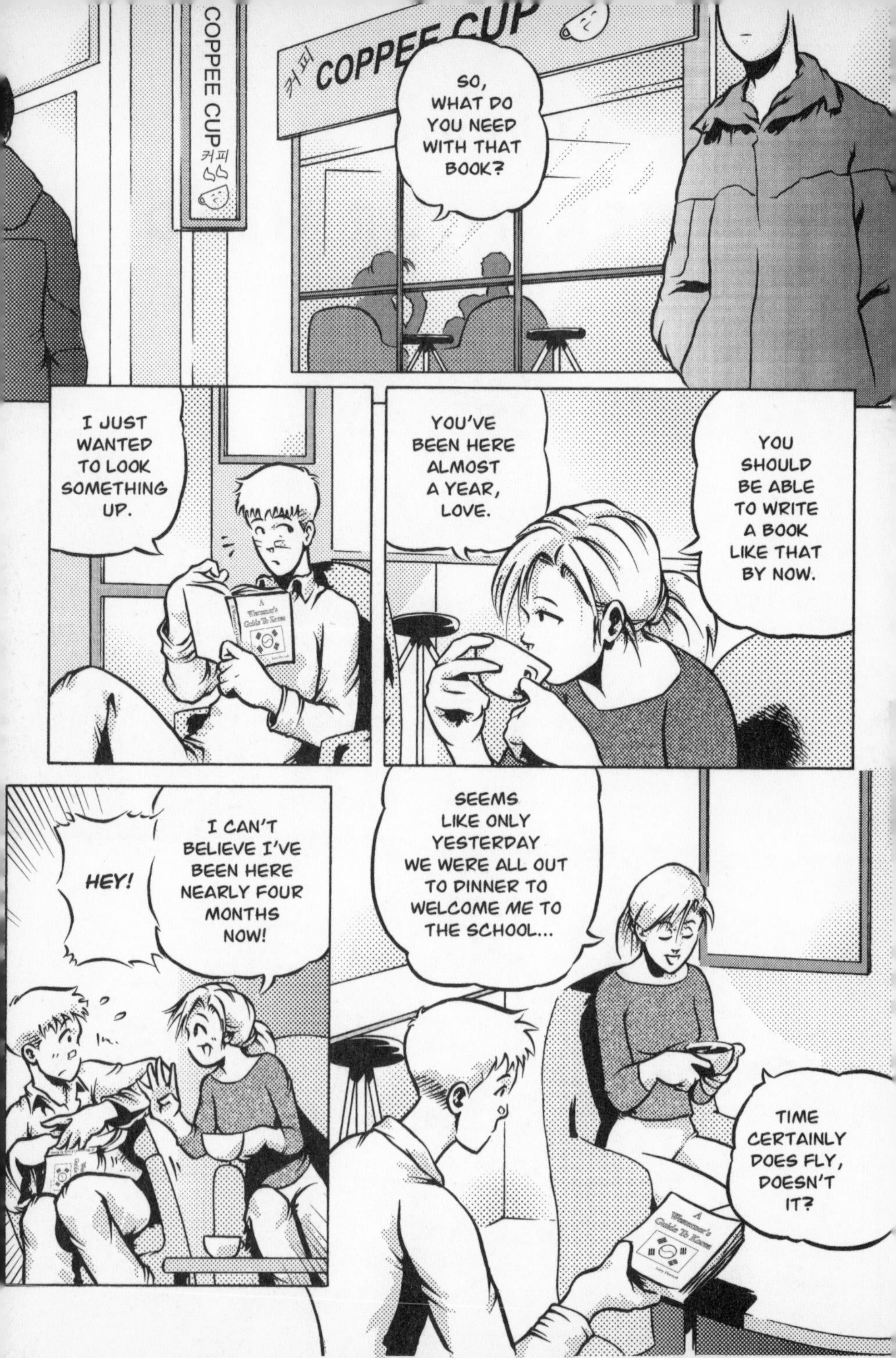
커피 COPPEE CUP
COPPEE CUP 커피
SO, WHAT DO YOU NEED WITH THAT BOOK?
I JUST WANTED TO LOOK SOMETHING UP.
YOU'VE BEEN HERE ALMOST A YEAR, LOVE.
YOU SHOULD BE ABLE TO WRITE A BOOK LIKE THAT BY NOW.
HEY!
I CAN'T BELIEVE I'VE BEEN HERE NEARLY FOUR MONTHS NOW!
SEEMS LIKE ONLY YESTERDAY WE WERE ALL OUT TO DINNER TO WELCOME ME TO THE SCHOOL...
TIME CERTAINLY DOES FLY, DOESN'T IT?

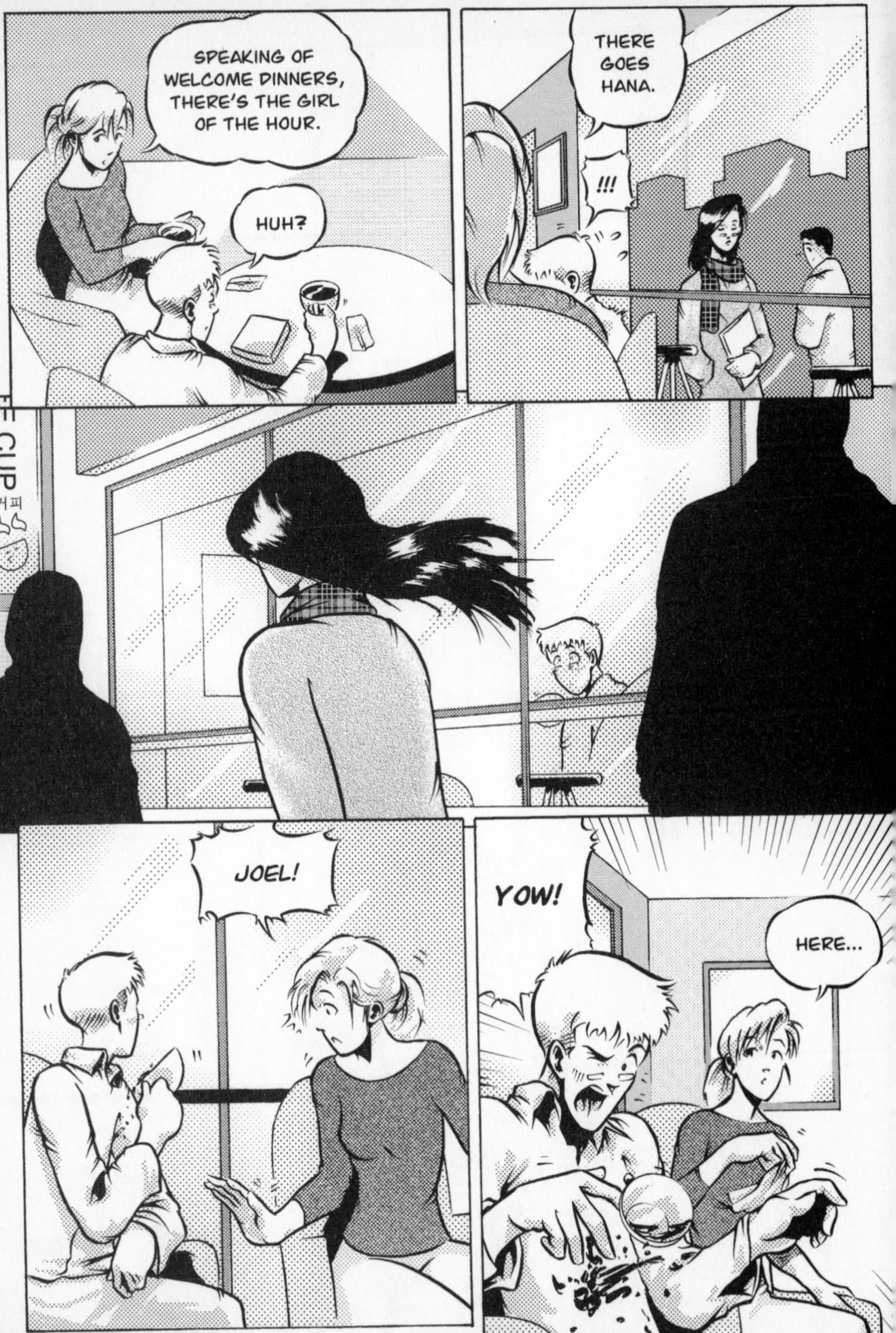
SPEAKING OF WELCOME DINNERS, THERE'S THE GIRL OF THE HOUR.
HUH?
THERE GOES HANA.
!!!
JOEL!
YOW!
HERE...

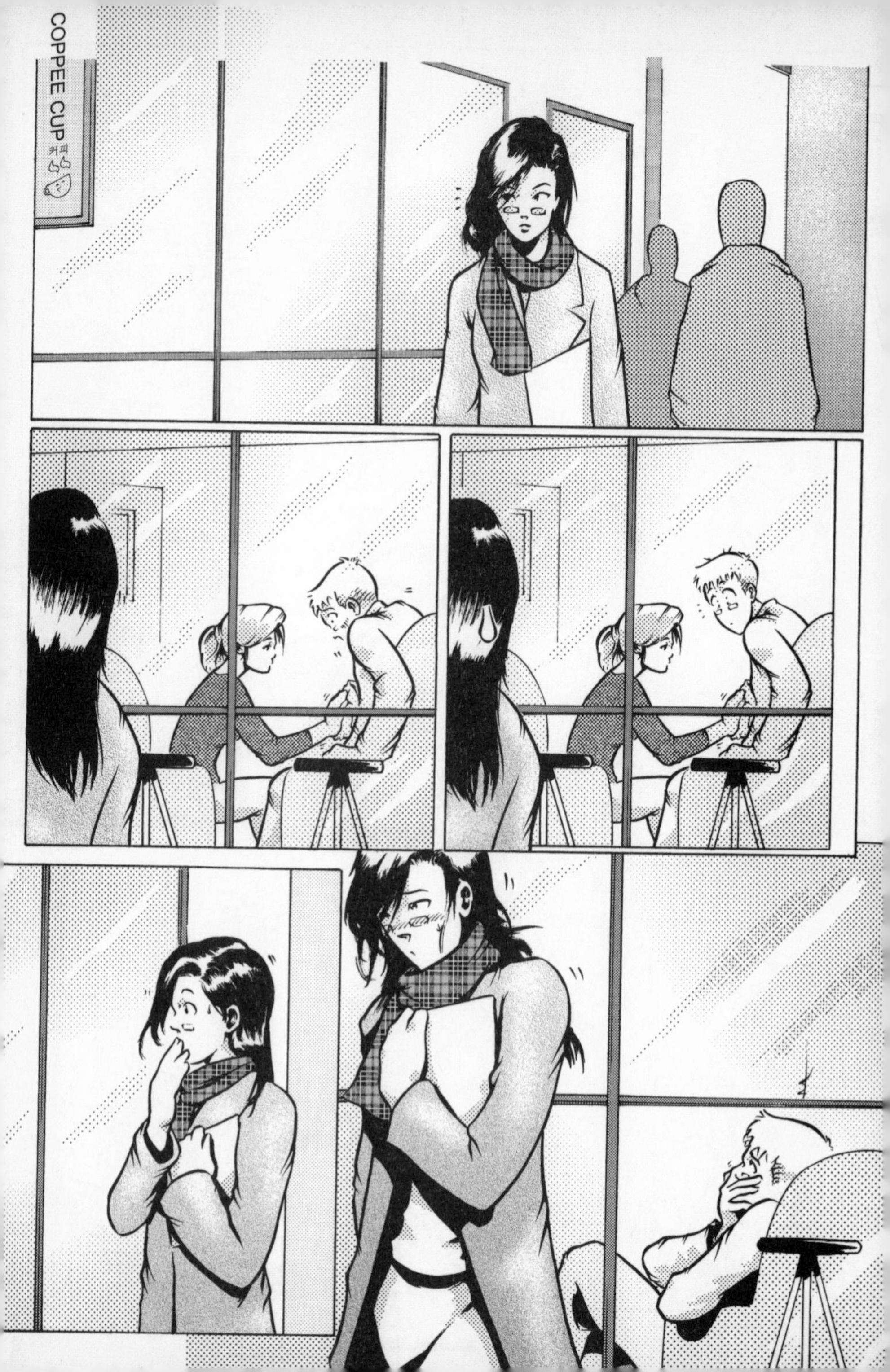
COPPEE CUP 커피

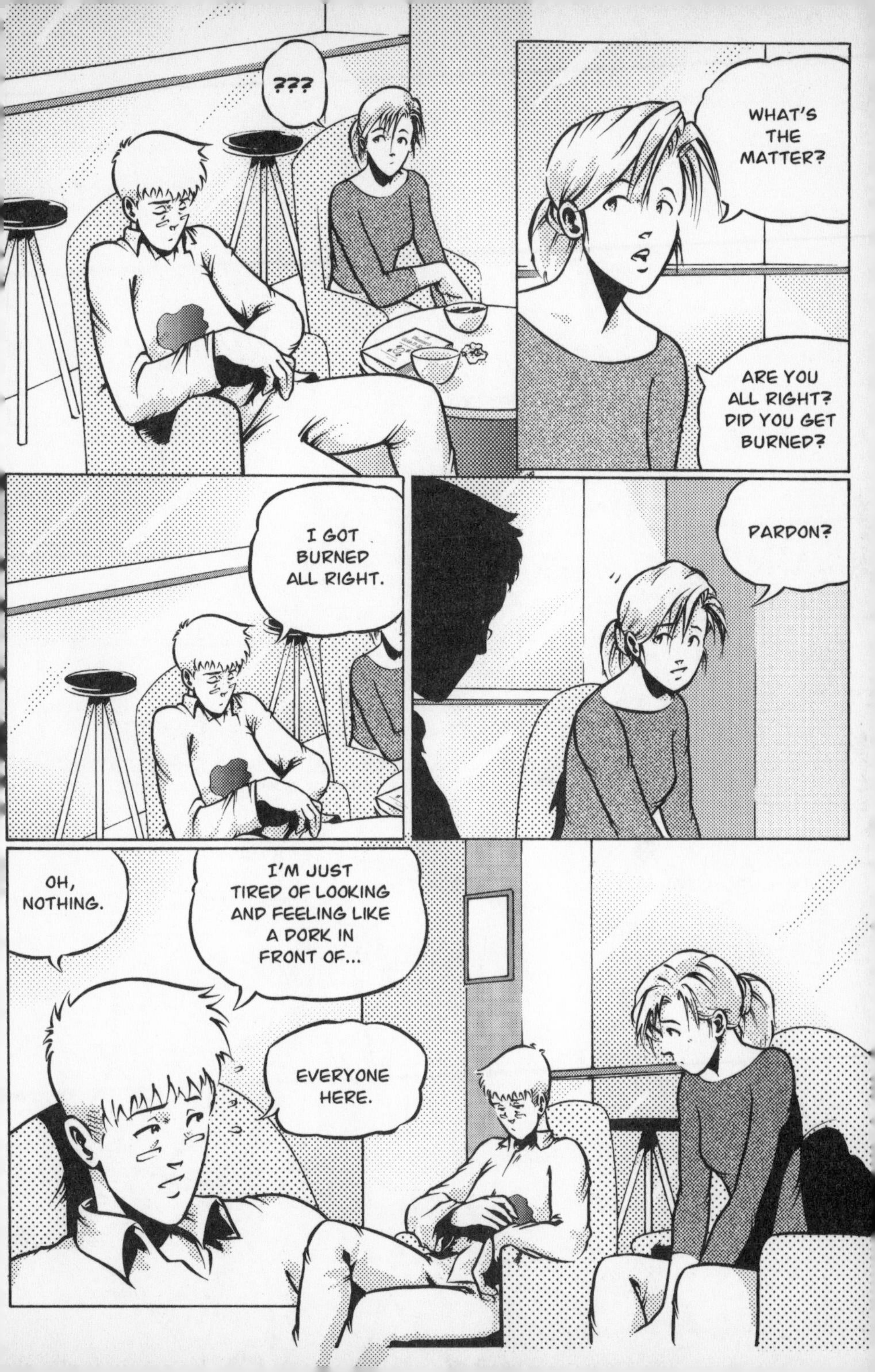
???
WHAT'S THE MATTER?
ARE YOU ALL RIGHT? DID YOU GET BURNED?
I GOT BURNED ALL RIGHT.
PARDON?
OH, NOTHING.
I'M JUST TIRED OF LOOKING AND FEELING LIKE A DORK IN FRONT OF...
EVERYONE HERE.

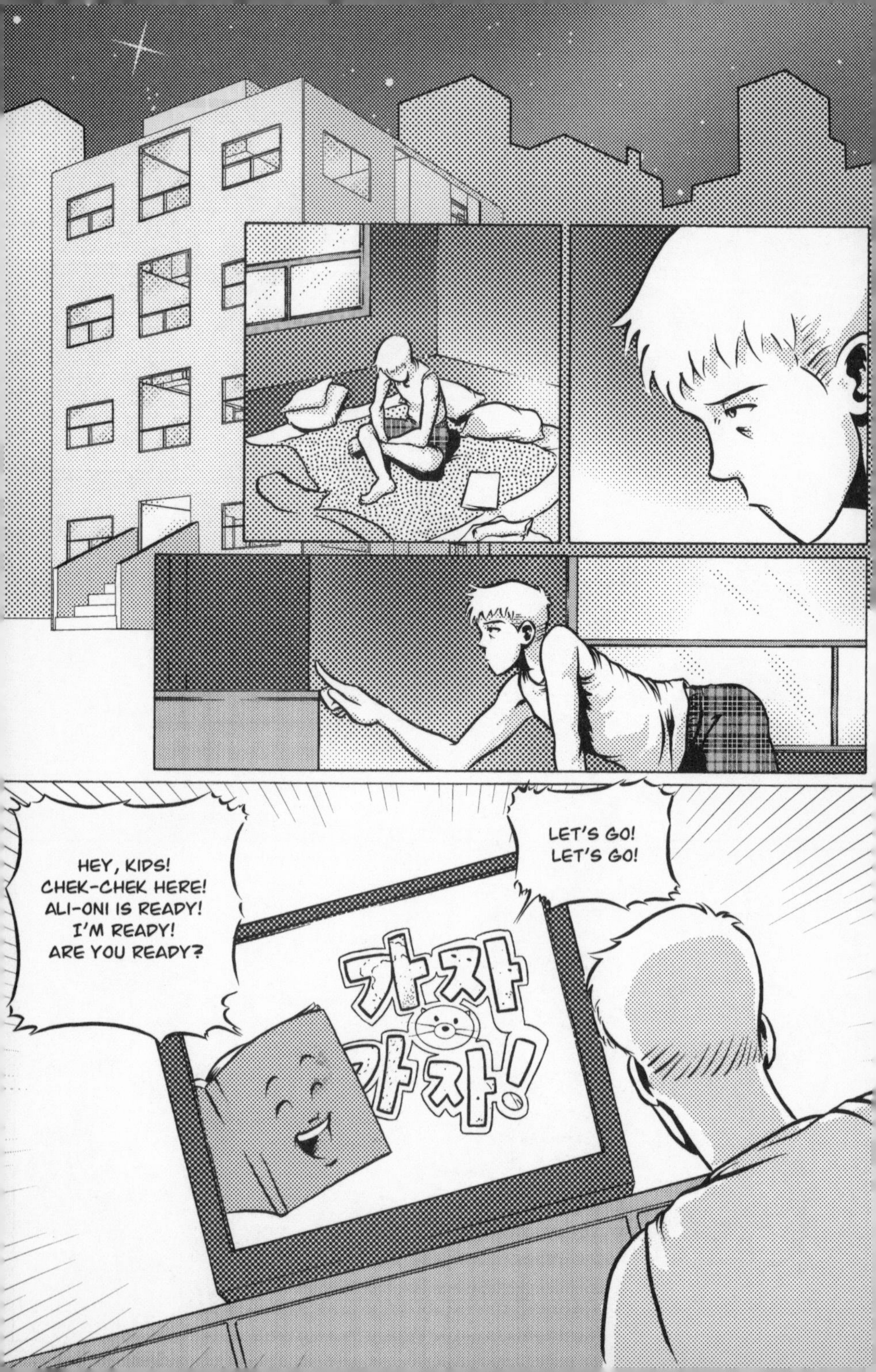
HEY, KIDS! CHEK-CHEK HERE! ALI-ONI IS READY! I'M READY! ARE YOU READY?
LET'S GO! LET'S GO!
가자 가자!

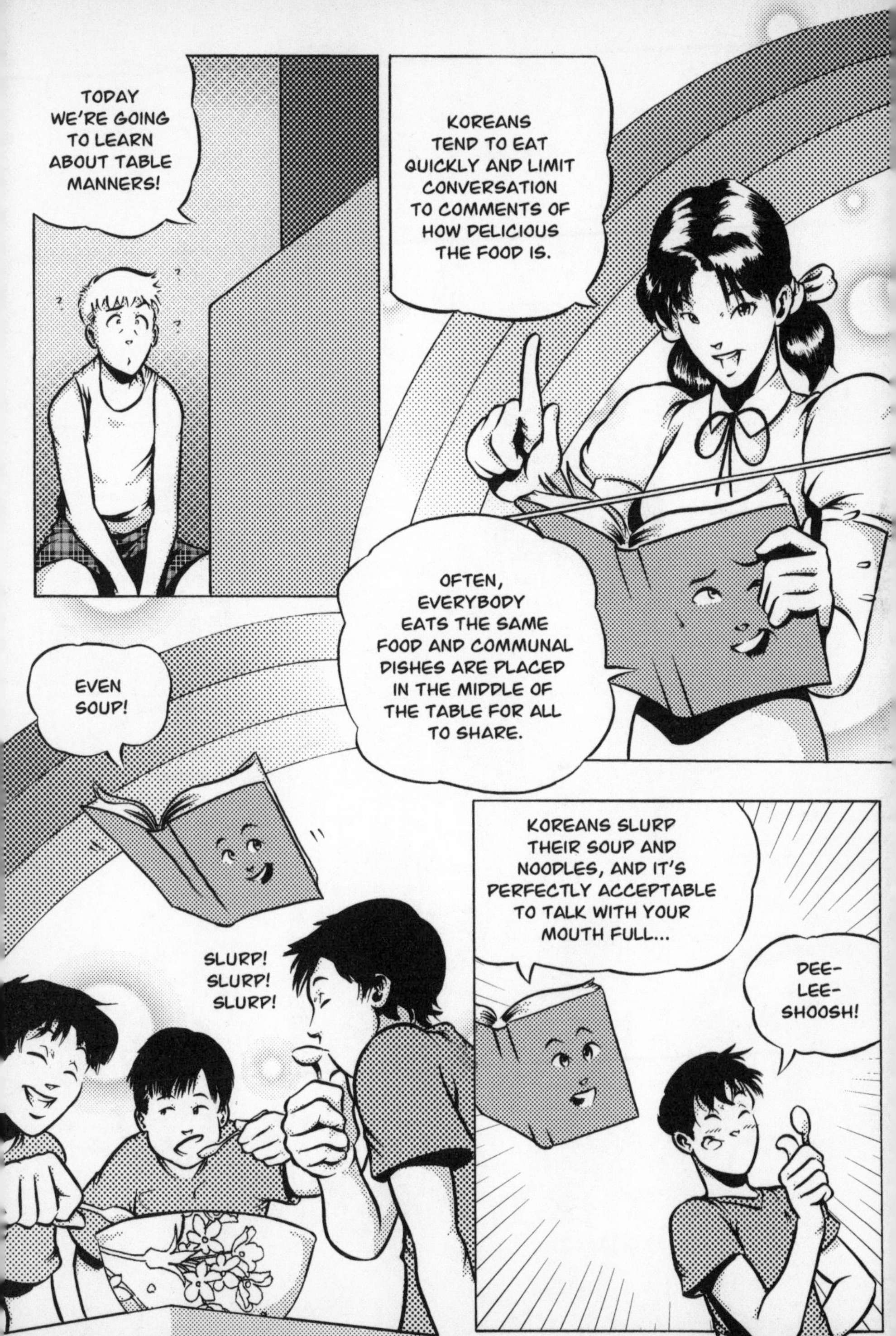
TODAY WE'RE GOING TO LEARN ABOUT TABLE MANNERS!
KOREANS TEND TO EAT QUICKLY AND LIMIT CONVERSATION TO COMMENTS OF HOW DELICIOUS THE FOOD IS.
OFTEN, EVERYBODY EATS THE SAME FOOD AND COMMUNAL DISHES ARE PLACED IN THE MIDDLE OF THE TABLE FOR ALL TO SHARE.
EVEN SOUP!
SLURP! SLURP! SLURP!
KOREANS SLURP THEIR SOUP AND NOODLES, AND IT'S PERFECTLY ACCEPTABLE TO TALK WITH YOUR MOUTH FULL...
DEE-LEE-SHOOSH!

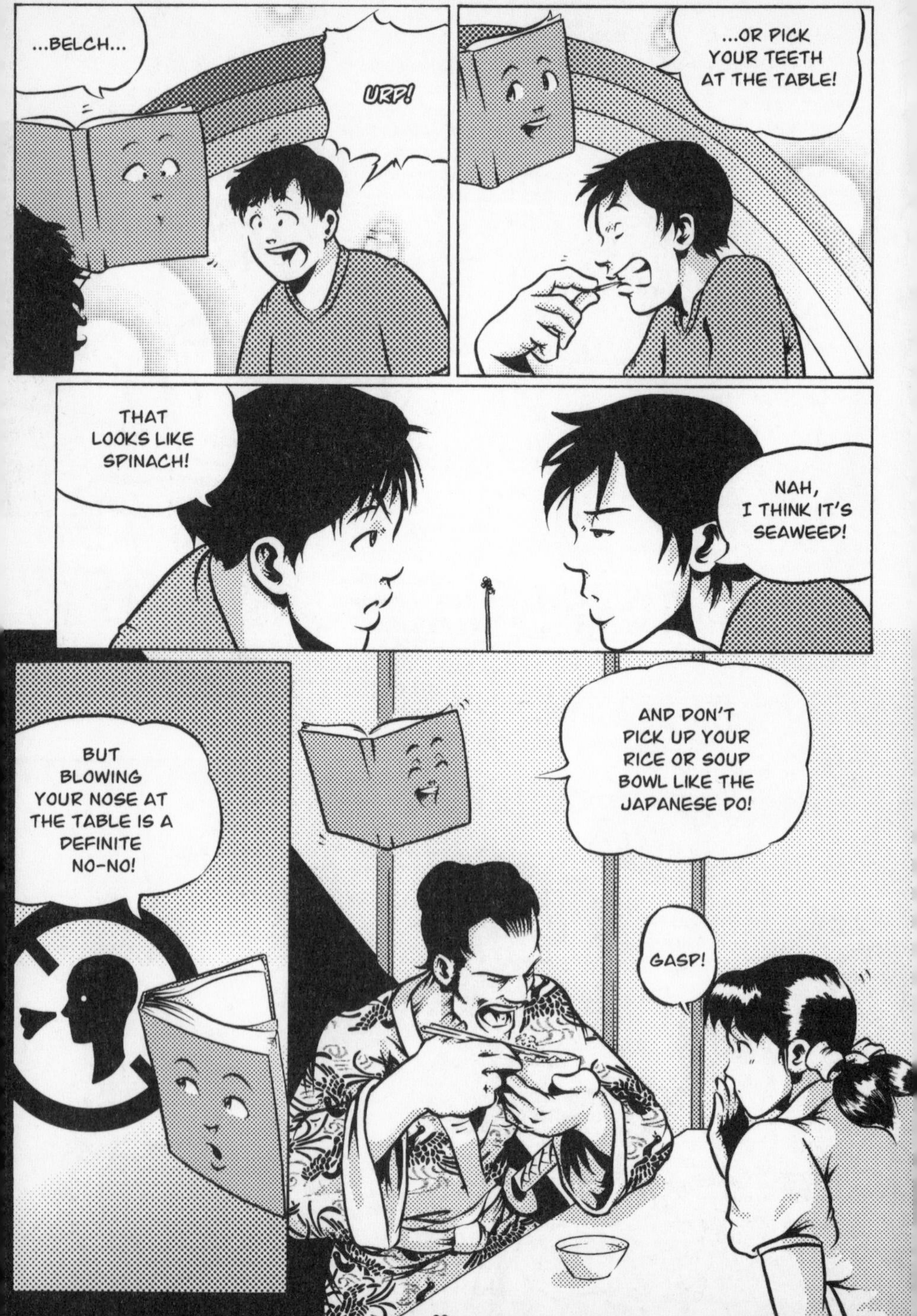
...BELCH...
URP!
...OR PICK YOUR TEETH AT THE TABLE!
THAT LOOKS LIKE SPINACH!
NAH, I THINK IT'S SEAWEED!
BUT BLOWING YOUR NOSE AT THE TABLE IS A DEFINITE NO-NO!
AND DON'T PICK UP YOUR RICE OR SOUP BOWL LIKE THE JAPANESE DO!
GASP!

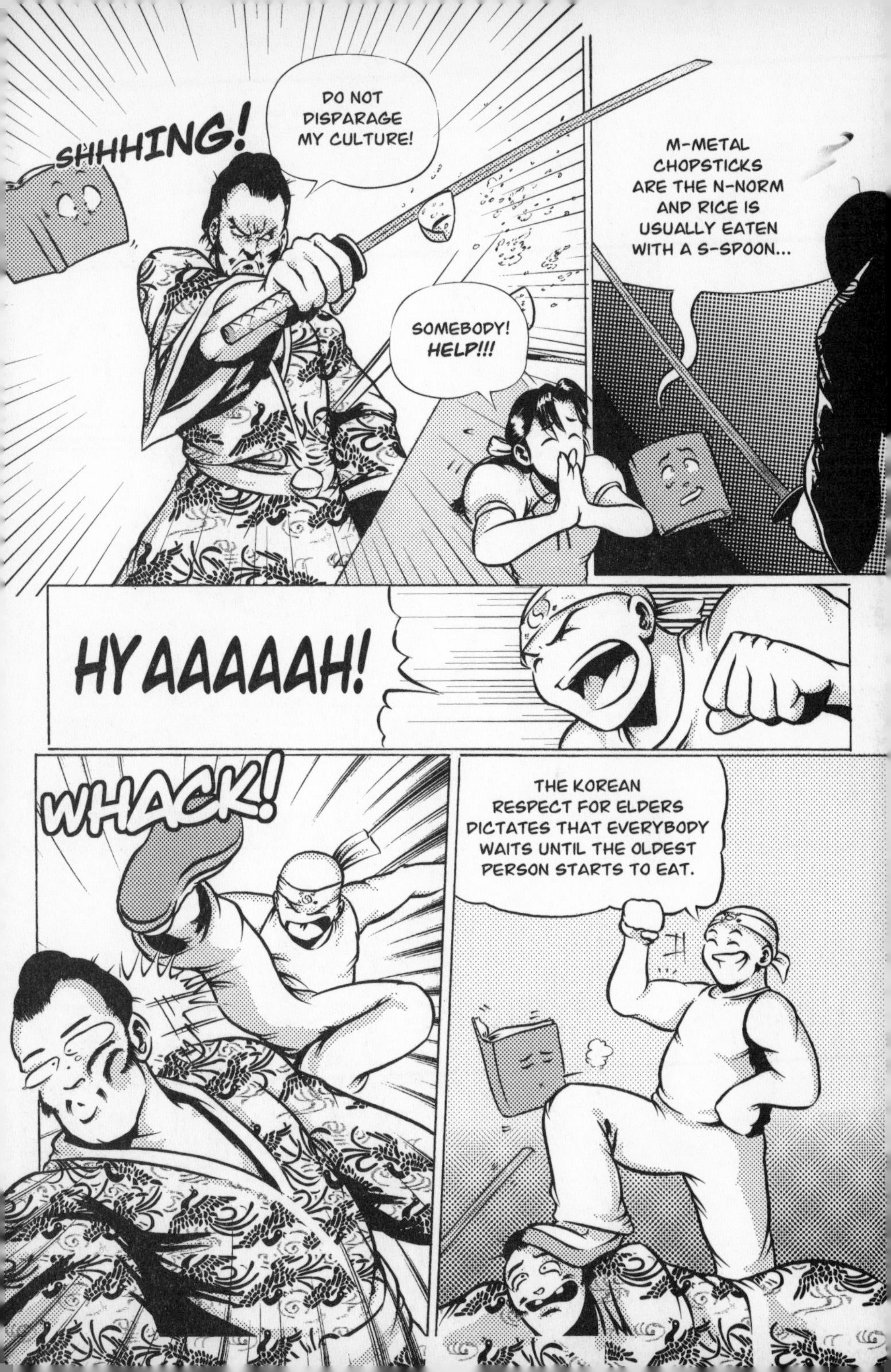
DO NOT DISPARAGE MY CULTURE!
SHHHING!
M-METAL CHOPSTICKS ARE THE N-NORM AND RICE IS USUALLY EATEN WITH A S-SPOON...
SOMEBODY! HELP!!!
HYAAAAAH!
WHACK!
THE KOREAN RESPECT FOR ELDERS DICTATES THAT EVERYBODY WAITS UNTIL THE OLDEST PERSON STARTS TO EAT.

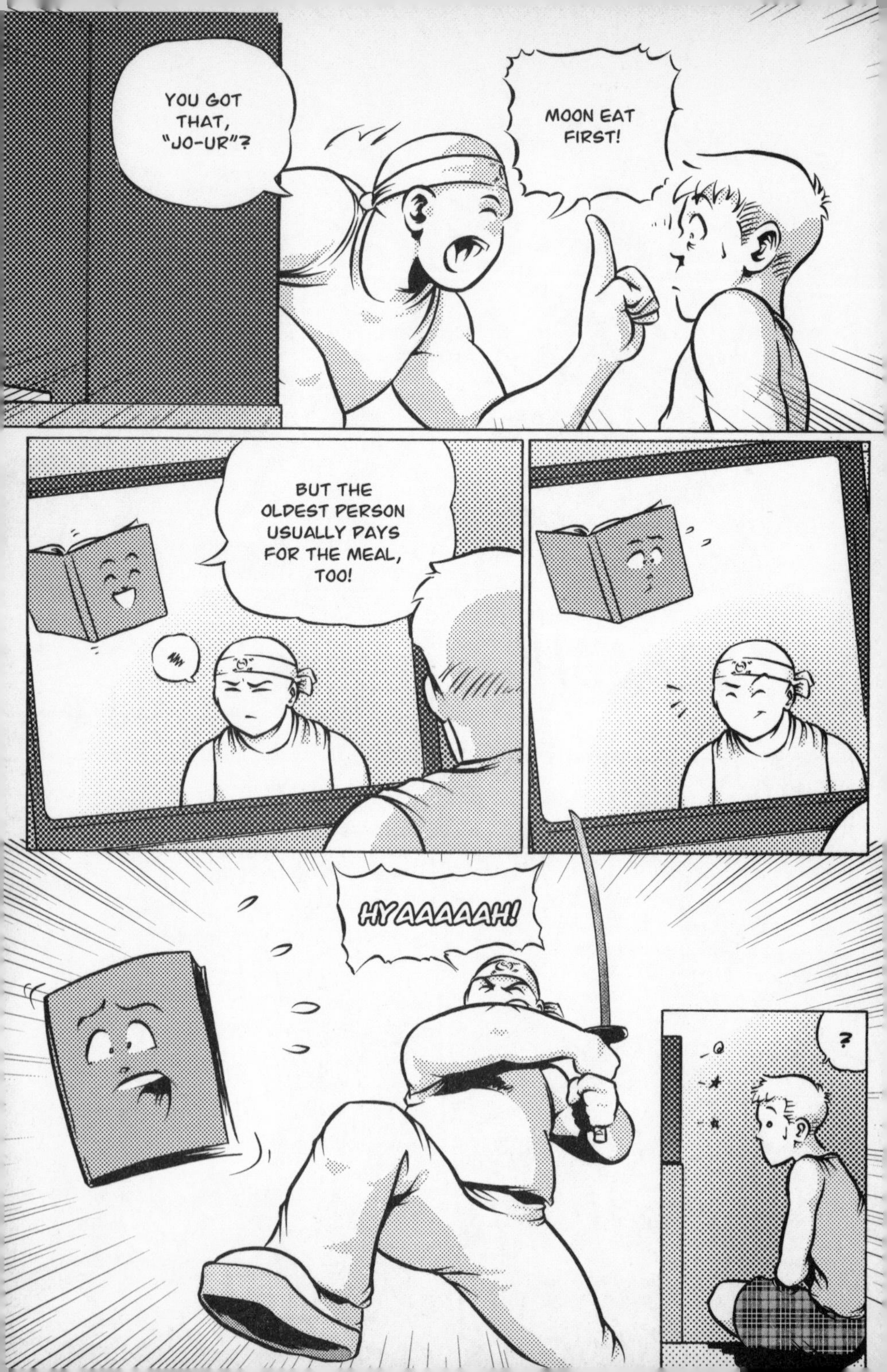
YOU GOT THAT, "JO-UR"?
MOON EAT FIRST!
BUT THE OLDEST PERSON USUALLY PAYS FOR THE MEAL, TOO!
HYAAAAAH!
?

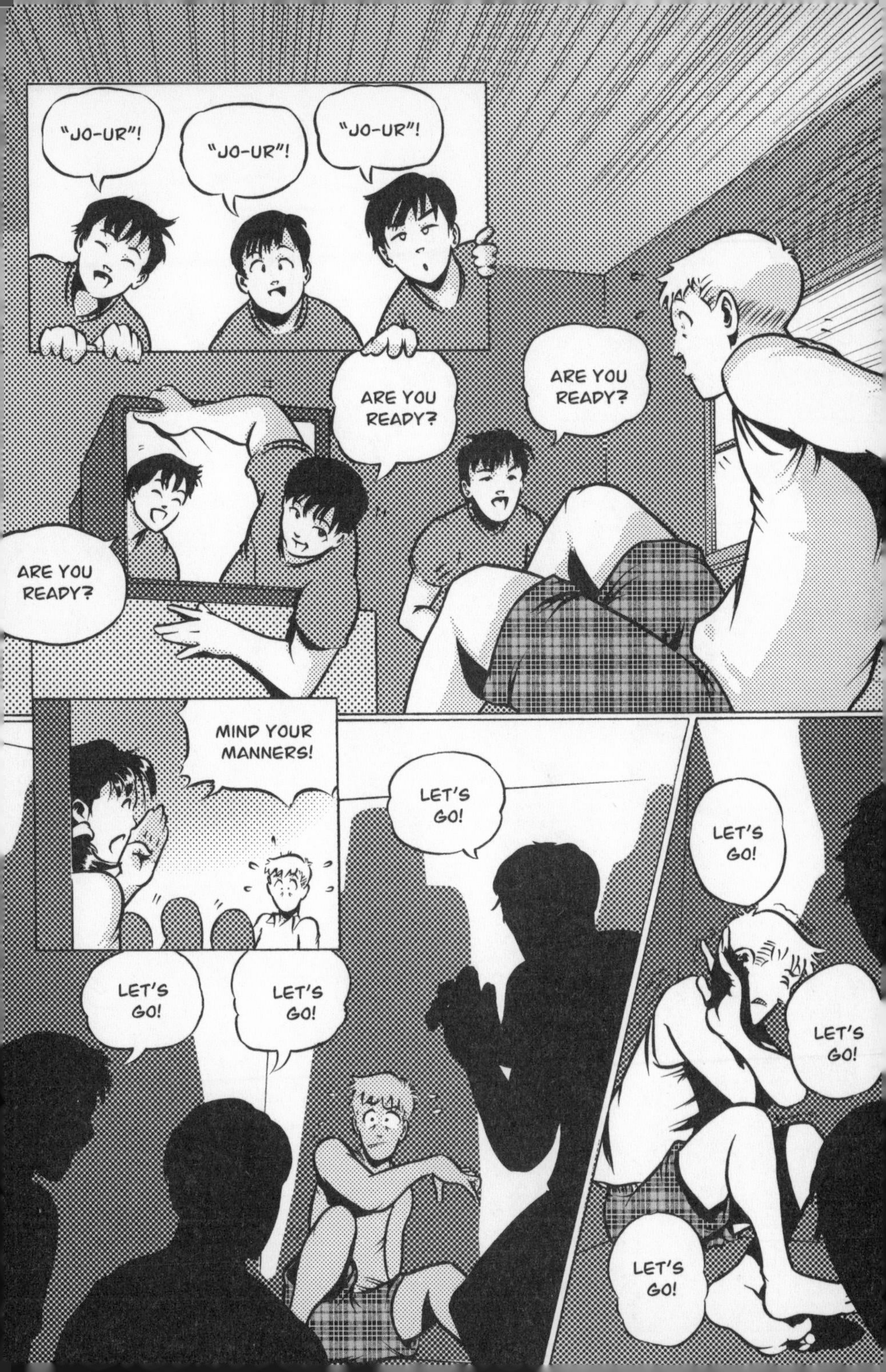
"JO-UR"!
"JO-UR"!
"JO-UR"!
ARE YOU READY?
ARE YOU READY?
ARE YOU READY?
MIND YOUR MANNERS!
LET'S GO!
LET'S GO!
LET'S GO!
LET'S GO!
LET'S GO!
LET'S GO!

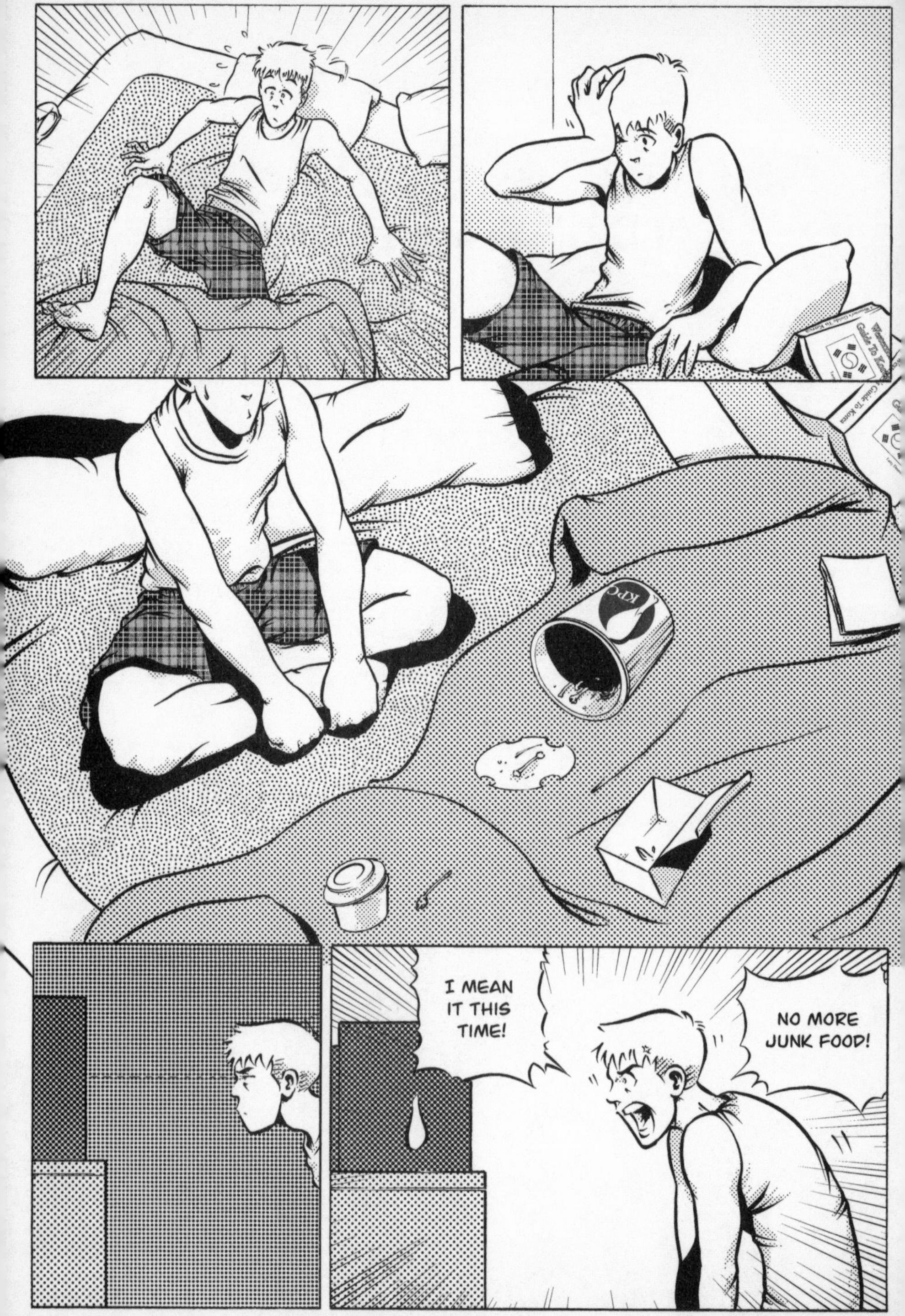
I MEAN IT THIS TIME!
NO MORE JUNK FOOD!

Chapter 12

JUST CALL MY NAME AND KALBI THERE

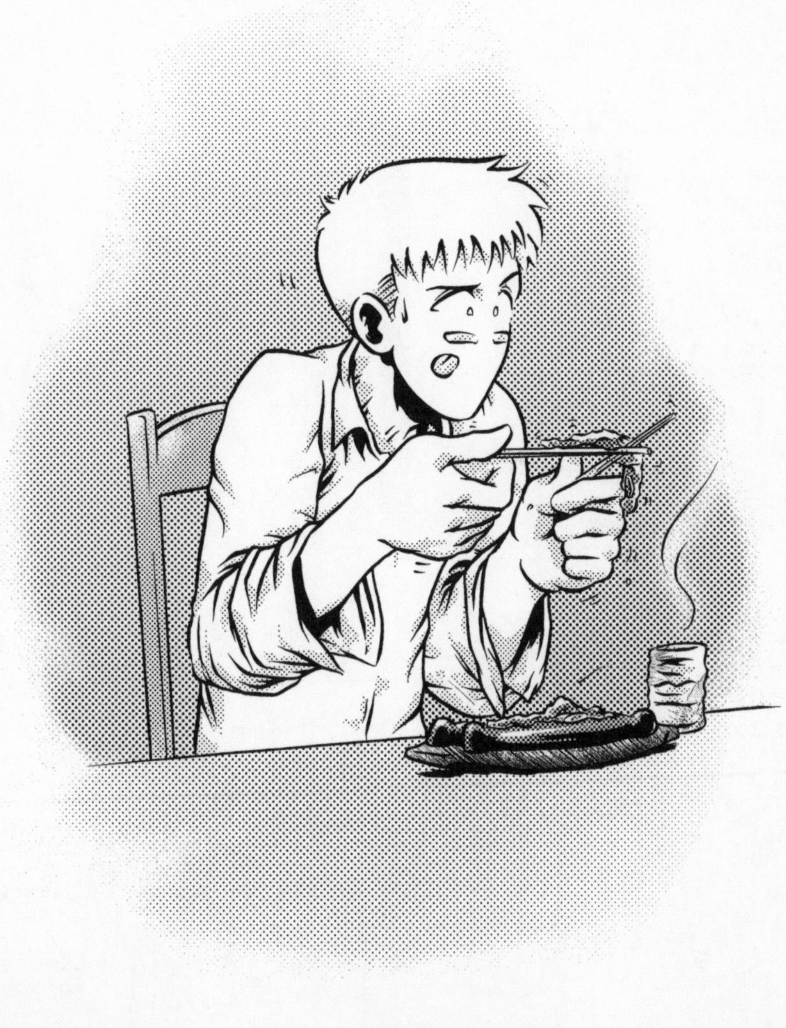

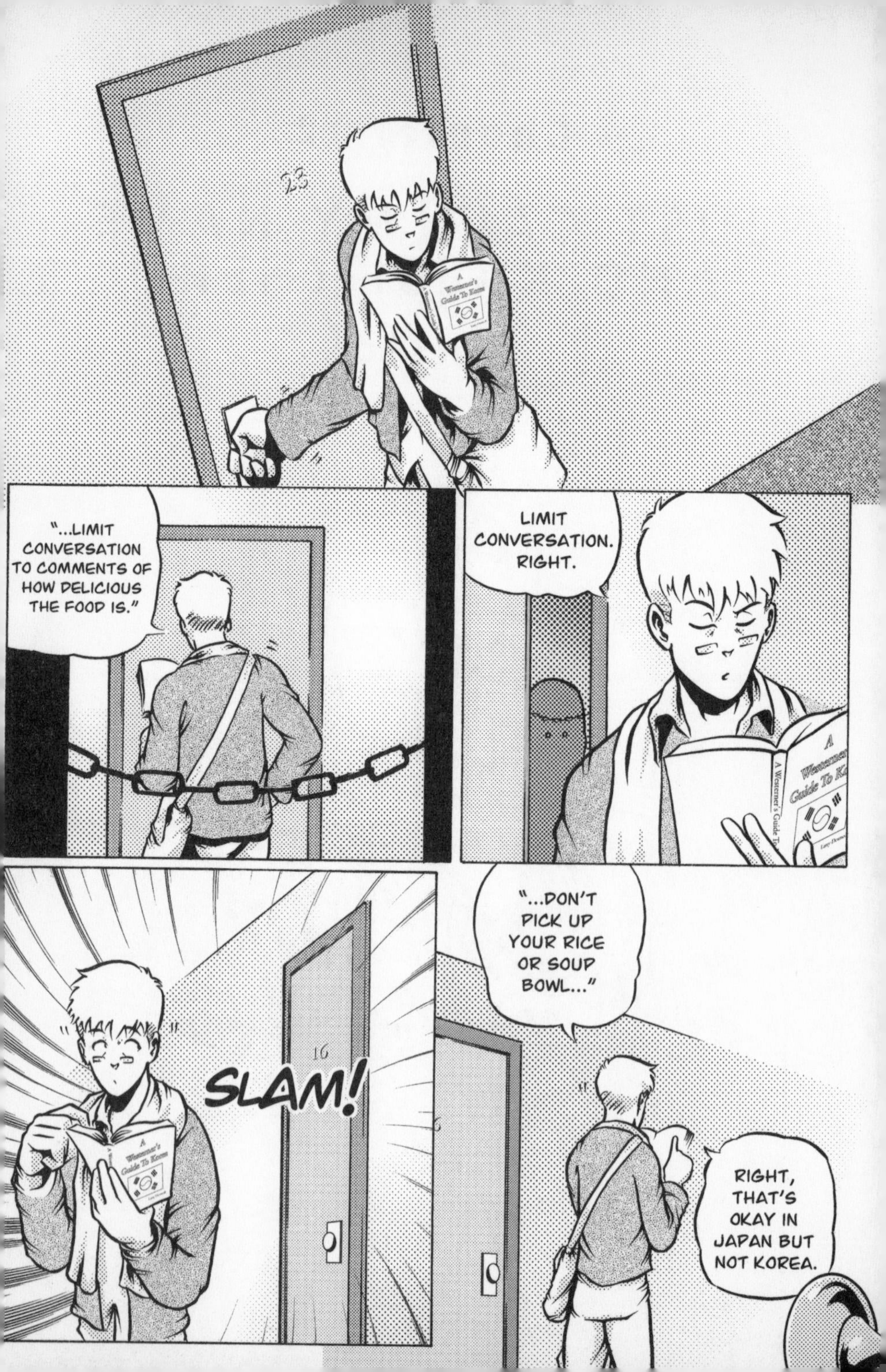

23
A Westerner's Guide To Korea
"...LIMIT CONVERSATION TO COMMENTS OF HOW DELICIOUS THE FOOD IS."
LIMIT CONVERSATION. RIGHT.
A Westerner's Guide To Korea
SLAM!
16
A Westerner's Guide To Korea
"...DON'T PICK UP YOUR RICE OR SOUP BOWL..."
RIGHT, THAT'S OKAY IN JAPAN BUT NOT KOREA.

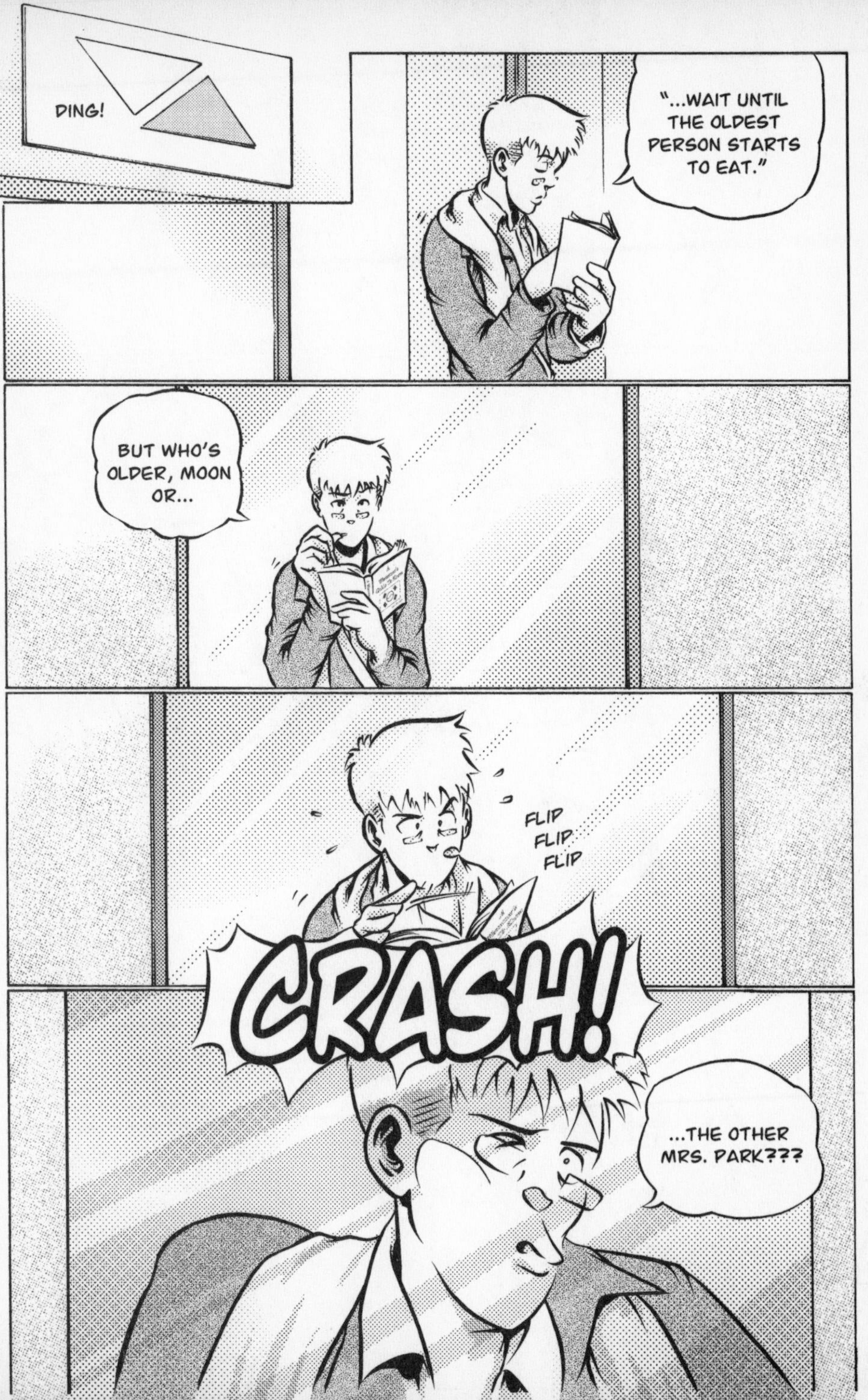
DING!
"...WAIT UNTIL THE OLDEST PERSON STARTS TO EAT."
BUT WHO'S OLDER, MOON OR...
FLIP FLIP FLIP
CRASH!
...THE OTHER MRS. PARK???

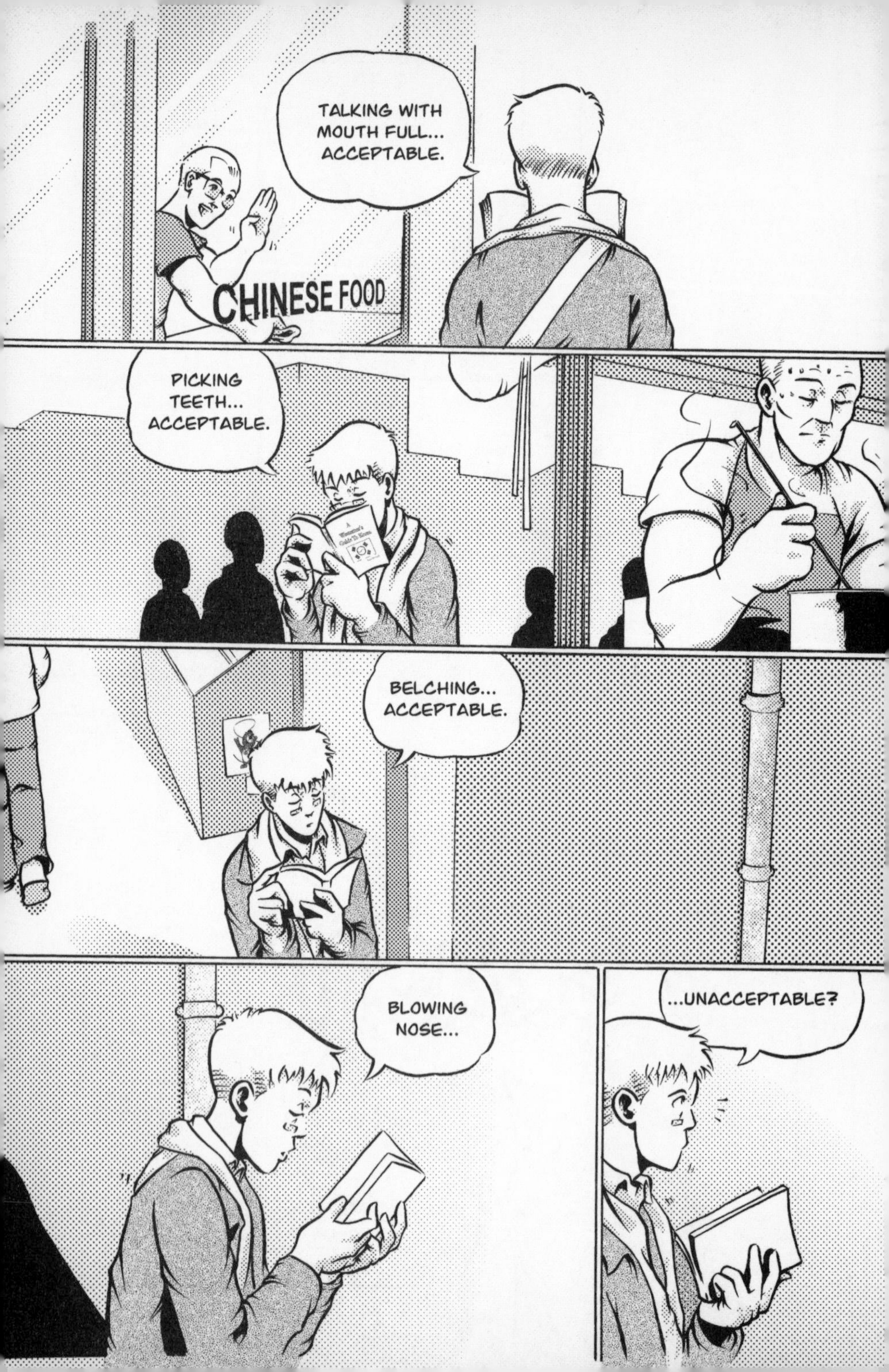
TALKING WITH MOUTH FULL... ACCEPTABLE.
CHINESE FOOD
PICKING TEETH... ACCEPTABLE.
BELCHING... ACCEPTABLE.
BLOWING NOSE...
...UNACCEPTABLE?

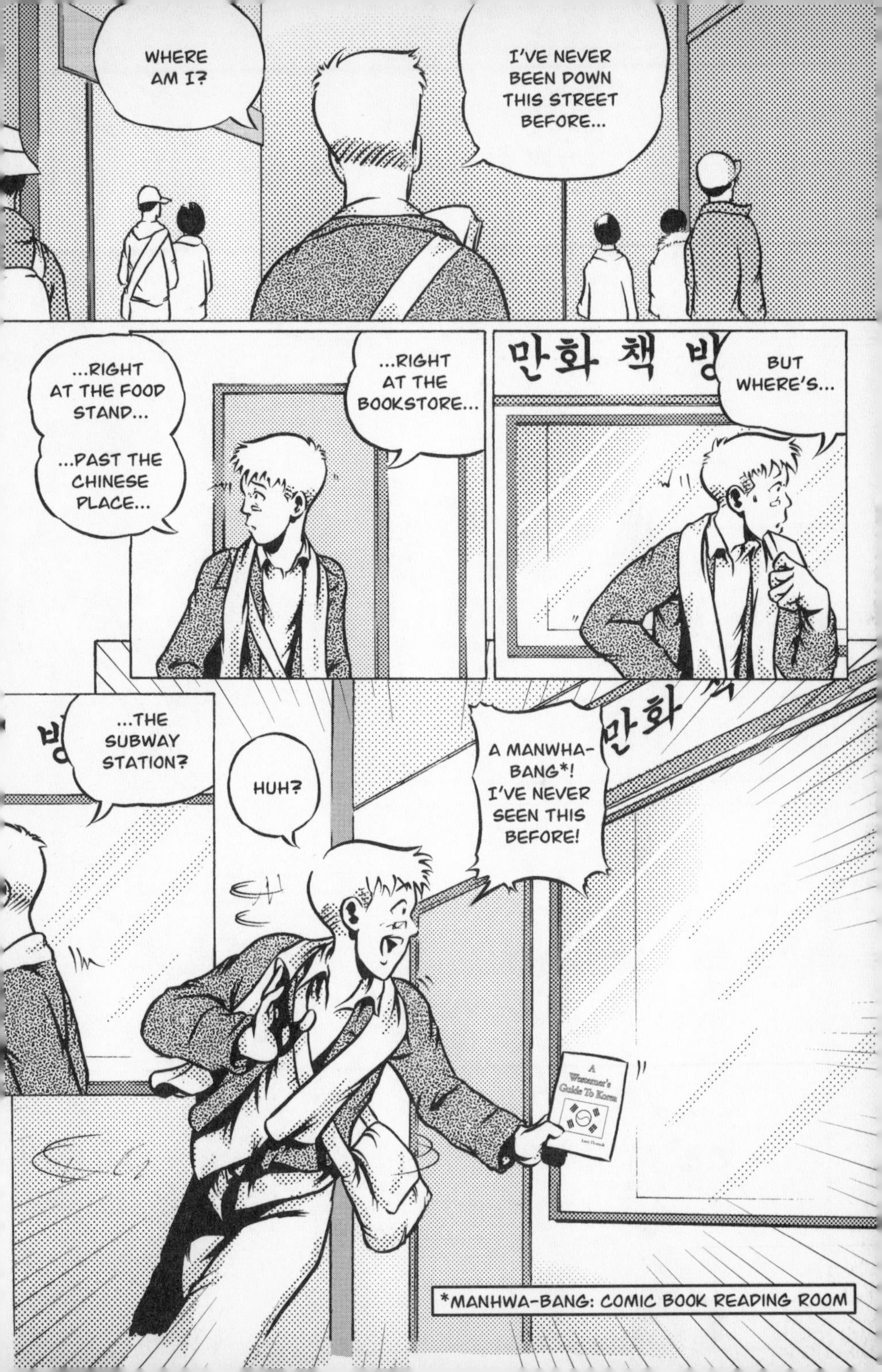
WHERE AM I?
I'VE NEVER BEEN DOWN THIS STREET BEFORE...
...RIGHT AT THE FOOD STAND...
...PAST THE CHINESE PLACE...
...RIGHT AT THE BOOKSTORE...
만화 책 방
BUT WHERE'S...
...THE SUBWAY STATION?
HUH?
만화
A MANWHA-BANG*! I'VE NEVER SEEN THIS BEFORE!
A Westerner's Guide To Korea
*MANHWA-BANG: COMIC BOOK READING ROOM

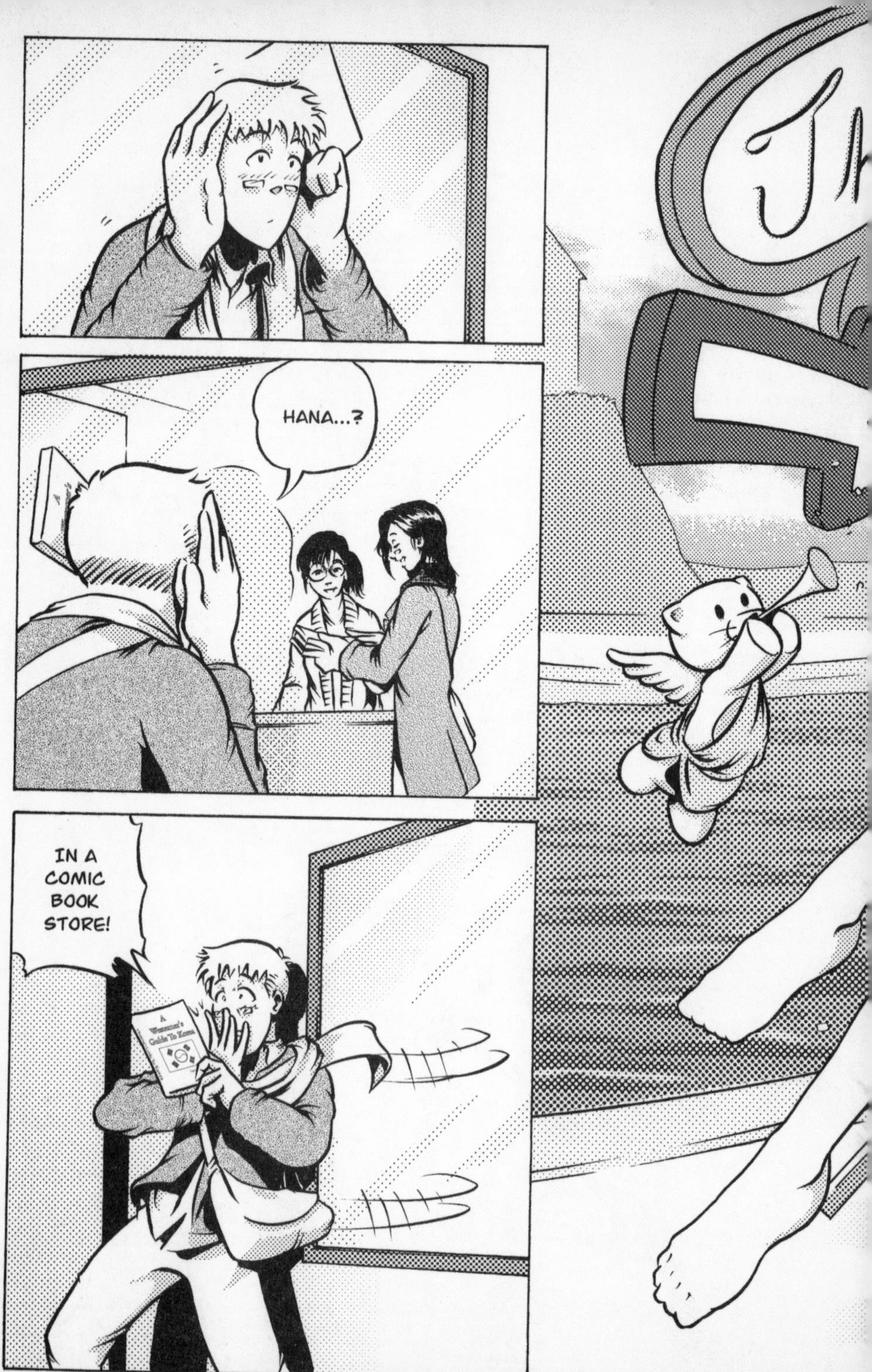
HANA...?
IN A COMIC BOOK STORE!
A Westerner's Guide To Korea

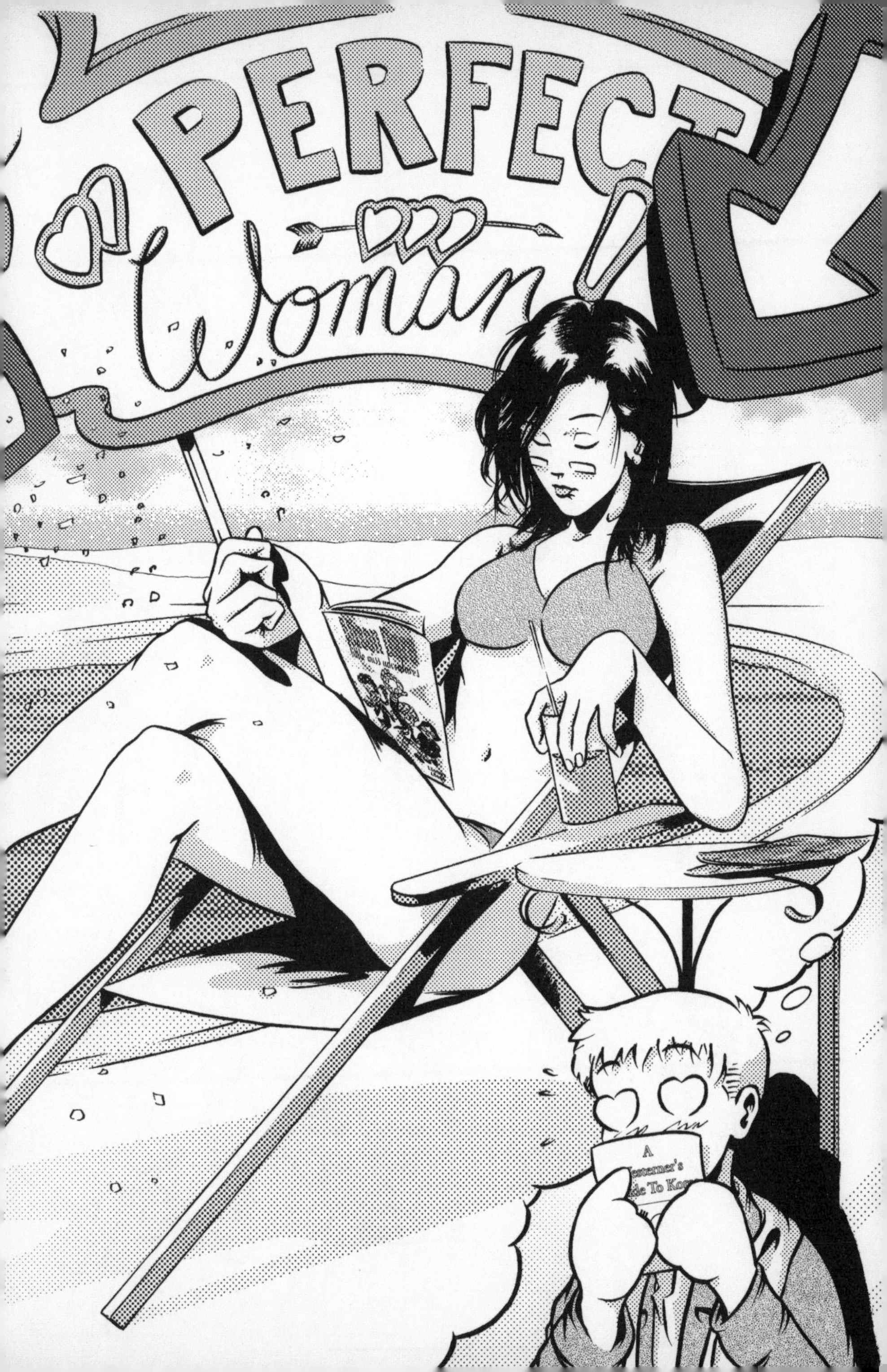
PERFECT
Woman
A
esterner's
ide To Kor

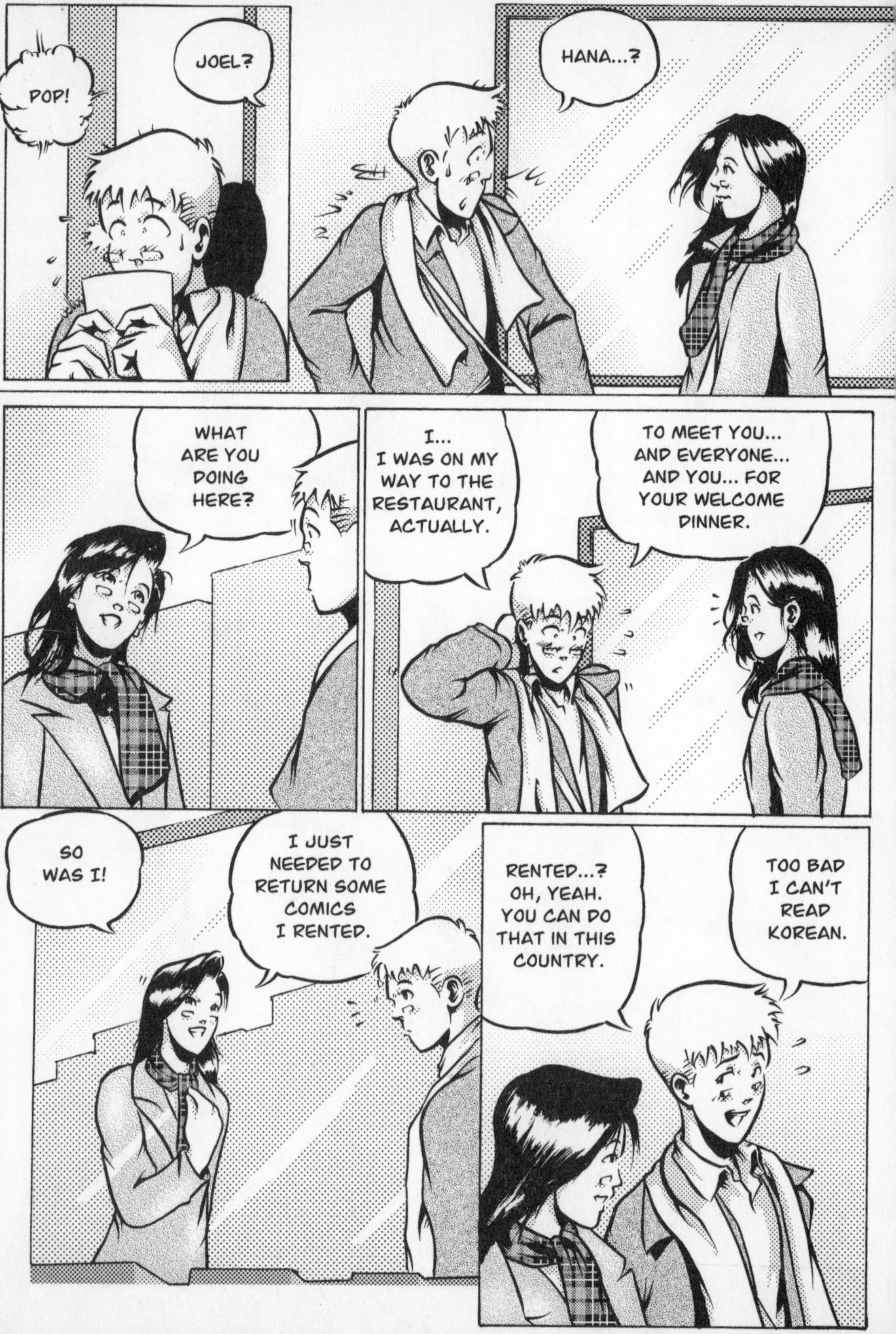
POP!
JOEL?
HANA...?
WHAT ARE YOU DOING HERE?
I... I WAS ON MY WAY TO THE RESTAURANT, ACTUALLY.
TO MEET YOU... AND EVERYONE... AND YOU... FOR YOUR WELCOME DINNER.
SO WAS I!
I JUST NEEDED TO RETURN SOME COMICS I RENTED.
RENTED...? OH, YEAH. YOU CAN DO THAT IN THIS COUNTRY.
TOO BAD I CAN'T READ KOREAN.

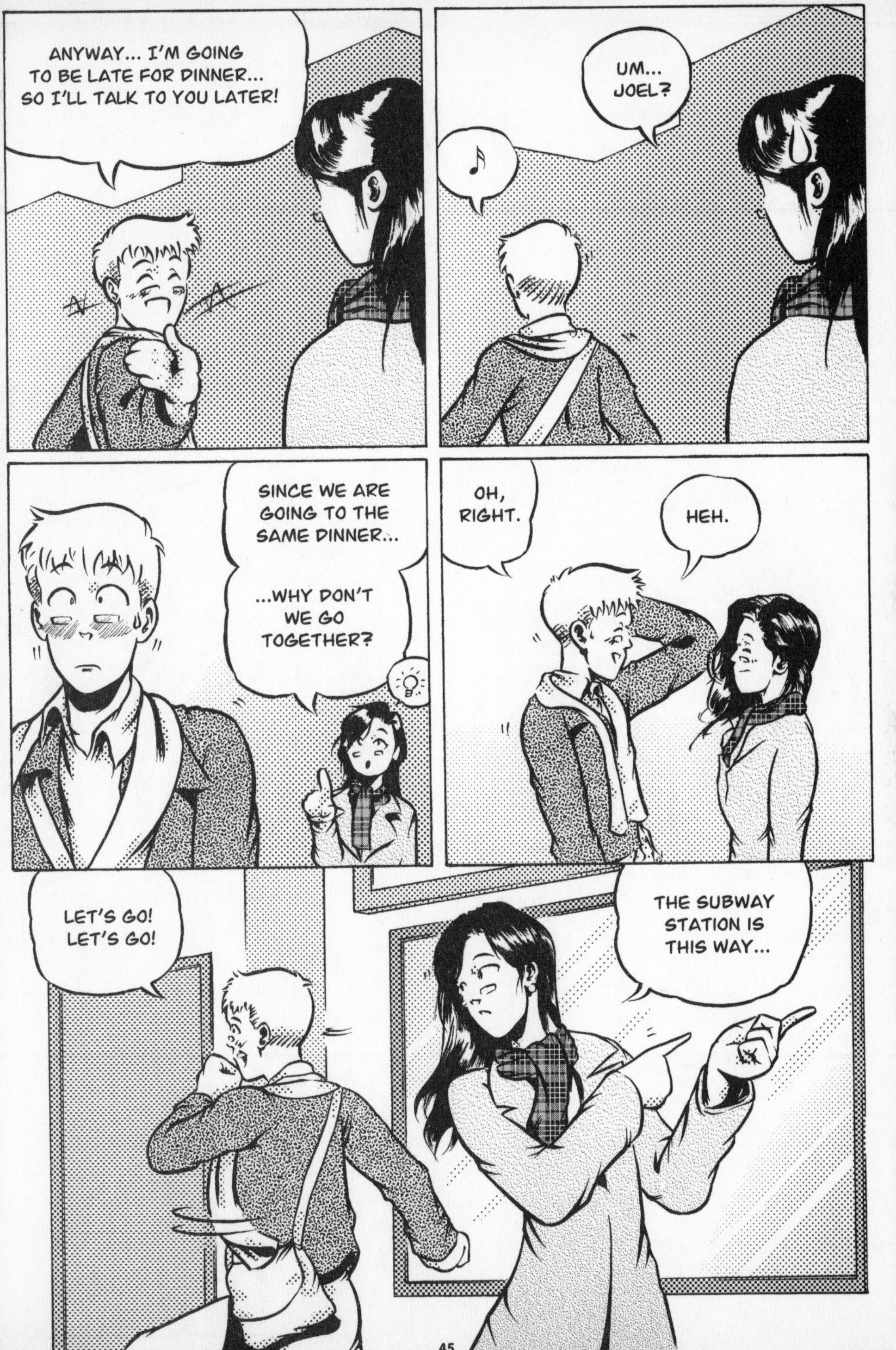
ANYWAY... I'M GOING TO BE LATE FOR DINNER... SO I'LL TALK TO YOU LATER!
UM... JOEL?
♪
SINCE WE ARE GOING TO THE SAME DINNER...
...WHY DON'T WE GO TOGETHER?
OH, RIGHT.
HEH.
LET'S GO! LET'S GO!
THE SUBWAY STATION IS THIS WAY...

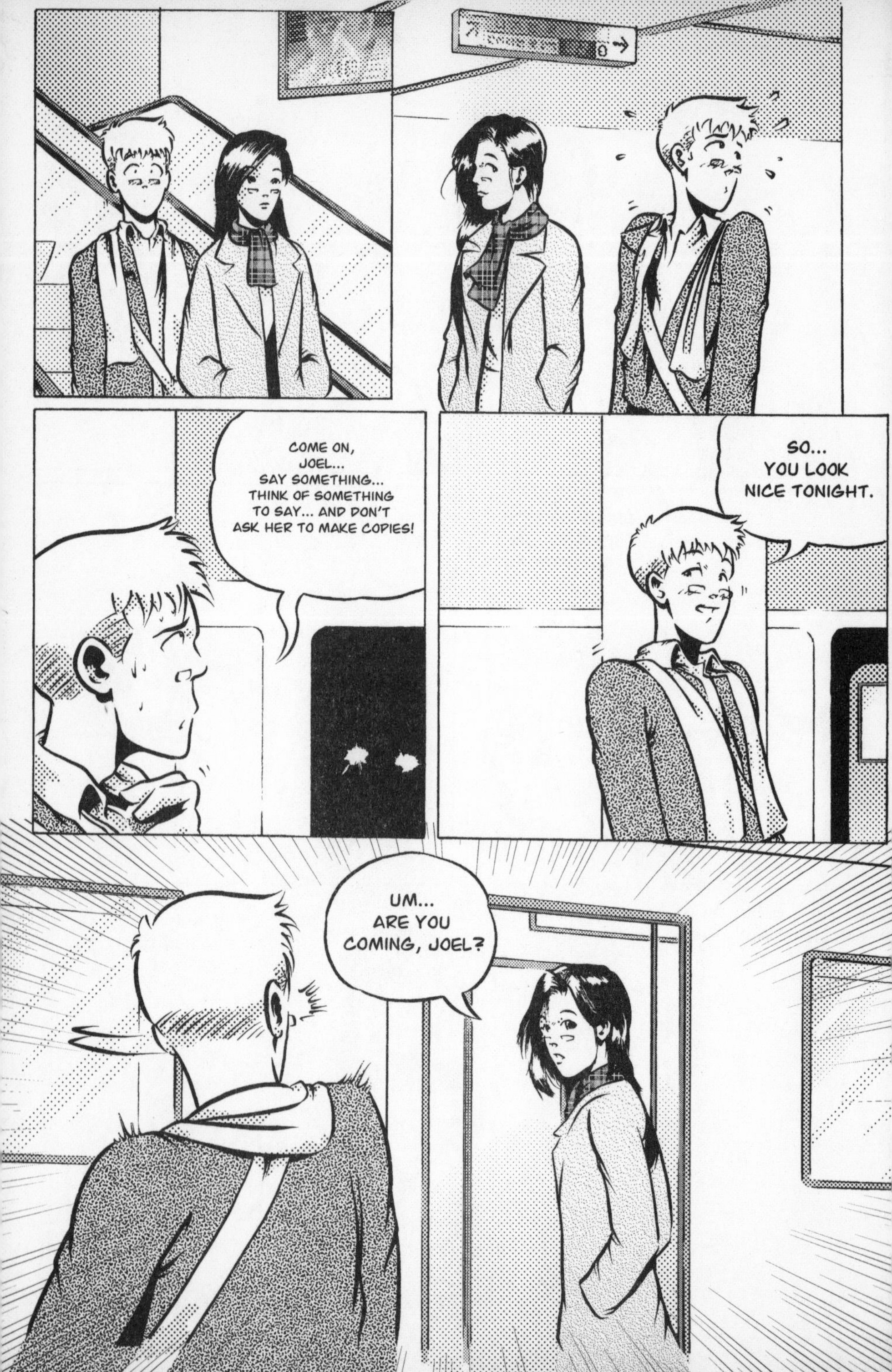
COME ON, JOEL... SAY SOMETHING... THINK OF SOMETHING TO SAY... AND DON'T ASK HER TO MAKE COPIES!
SO... YOU LOOK NICE TONIGHT.
UM... ARE YOU COMING, JOEL?

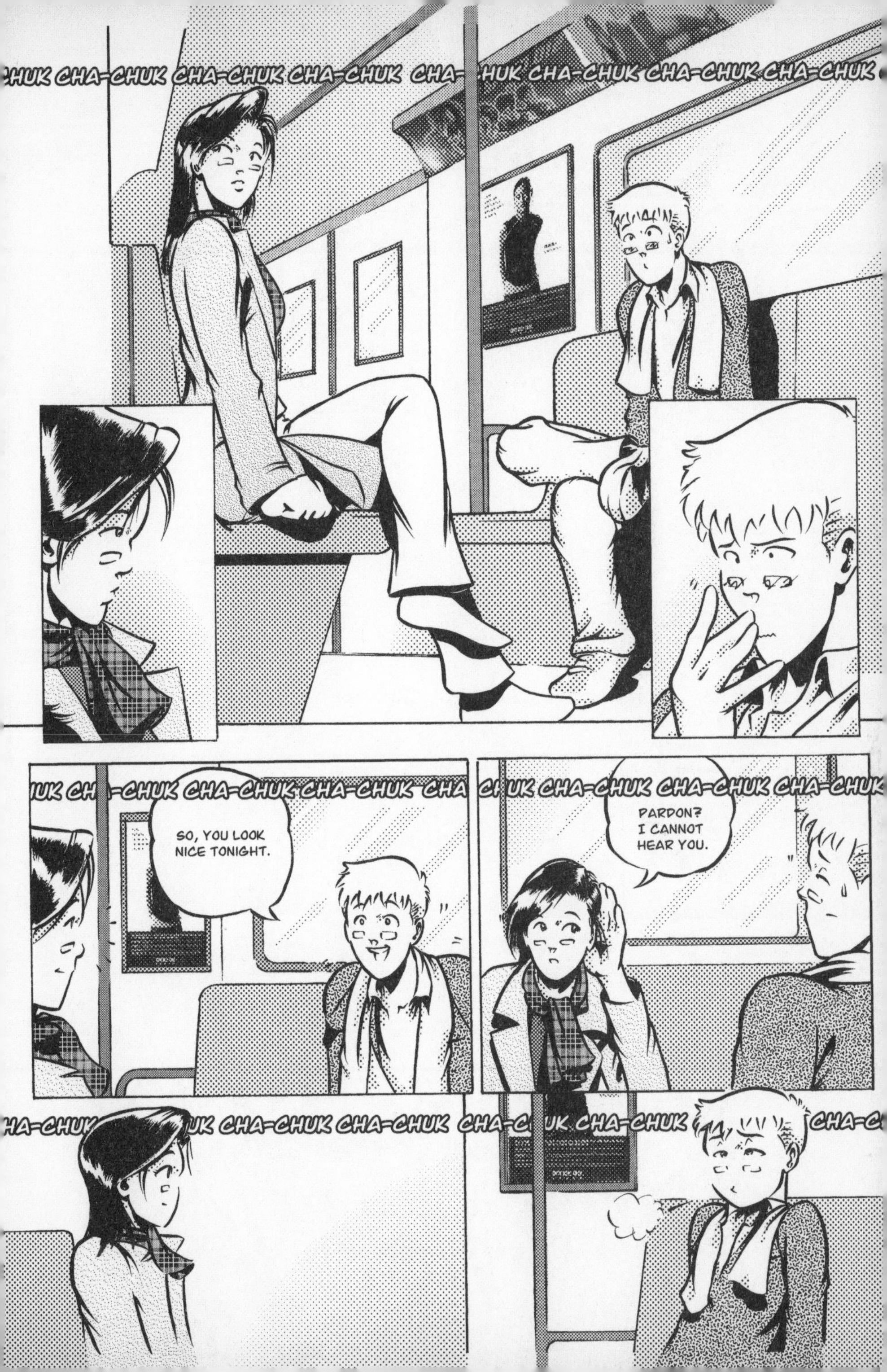
CHA-CHUK CHA-CHUK CHA-CHUK CHA-CHUK CHA-CHUK CHA-CHUK
CHA-CHUK CHA-CHUK CHA-CHUK CHA-CHUK CHA-CHUK
SO, YOU LOOK NICE TONIGHT.
PARDON? I CANNOT HEAR YOU.
CHA-CHUK CHA-CHUK CHA-CHUK CHA-CHUK CHA-CHUK

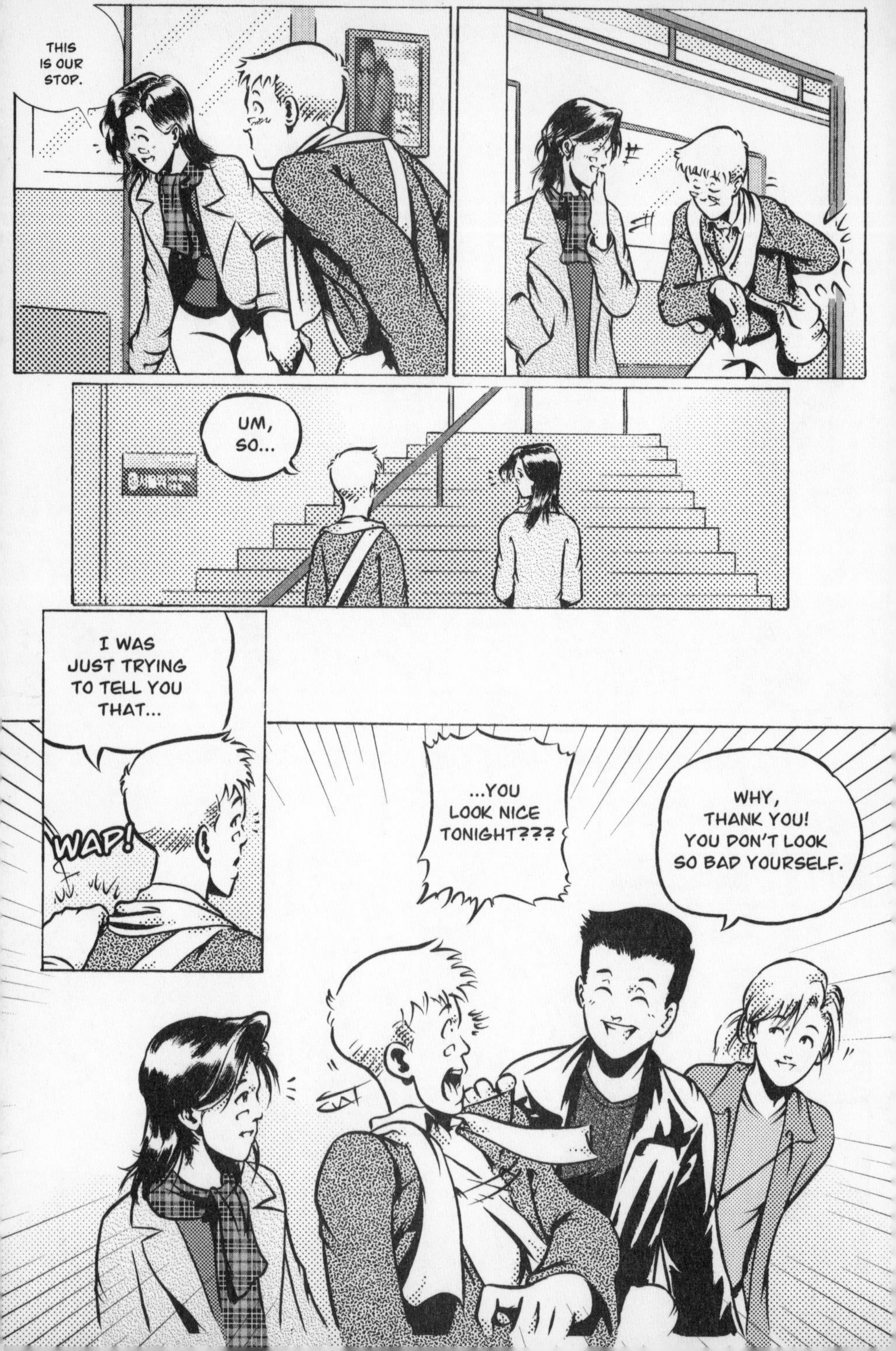
THIS IS OUR STOP.
UM, SO...
I WAS JUST TRYING TO TELL YOU THAT...
WAP!
...YOU LOOK NICE TONIGHT???
WHY, THANK YOU! YOU DON'T LOOK SO BAD YOURSELF.

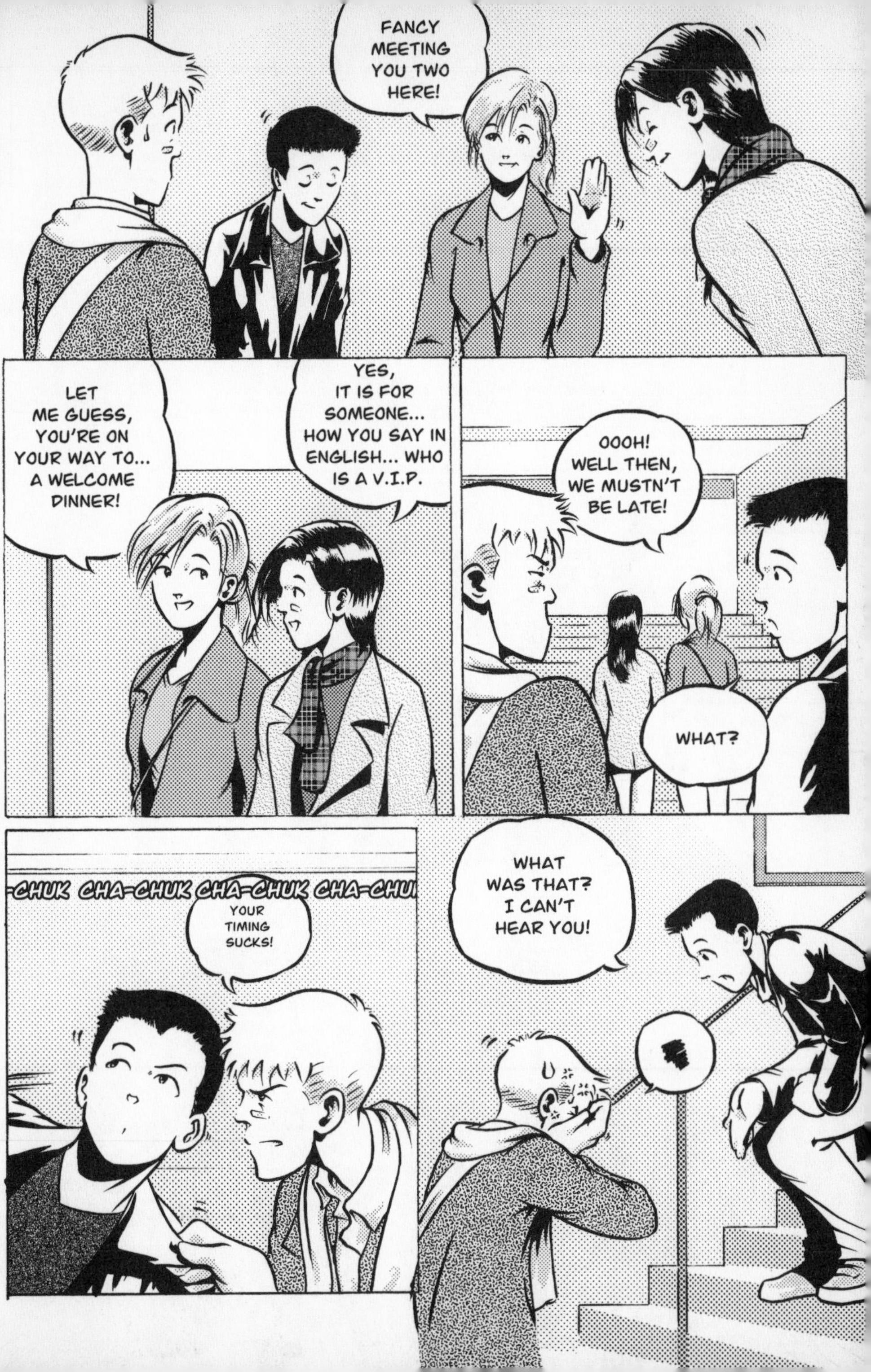
FANCY MEETING YOU TWO HERE!
LET ME GUESS, YOU'RE ON YOUR WAY TO... A WELCOME DINNER!
YES, IT IS FOR SOMEONE... HOW YOU SAY IN ENGLISH... WHO IS A V.I.P.
OOOH! WELL THEN, WE MUSTN'T BE LATE!
WHAT?
-CHUK CHA-CHUK CHA-CHUK CHA-CHU
YOUR TIMING SUCKS!
WHAT WAS THAT? I CAN'T HEAR YOU!

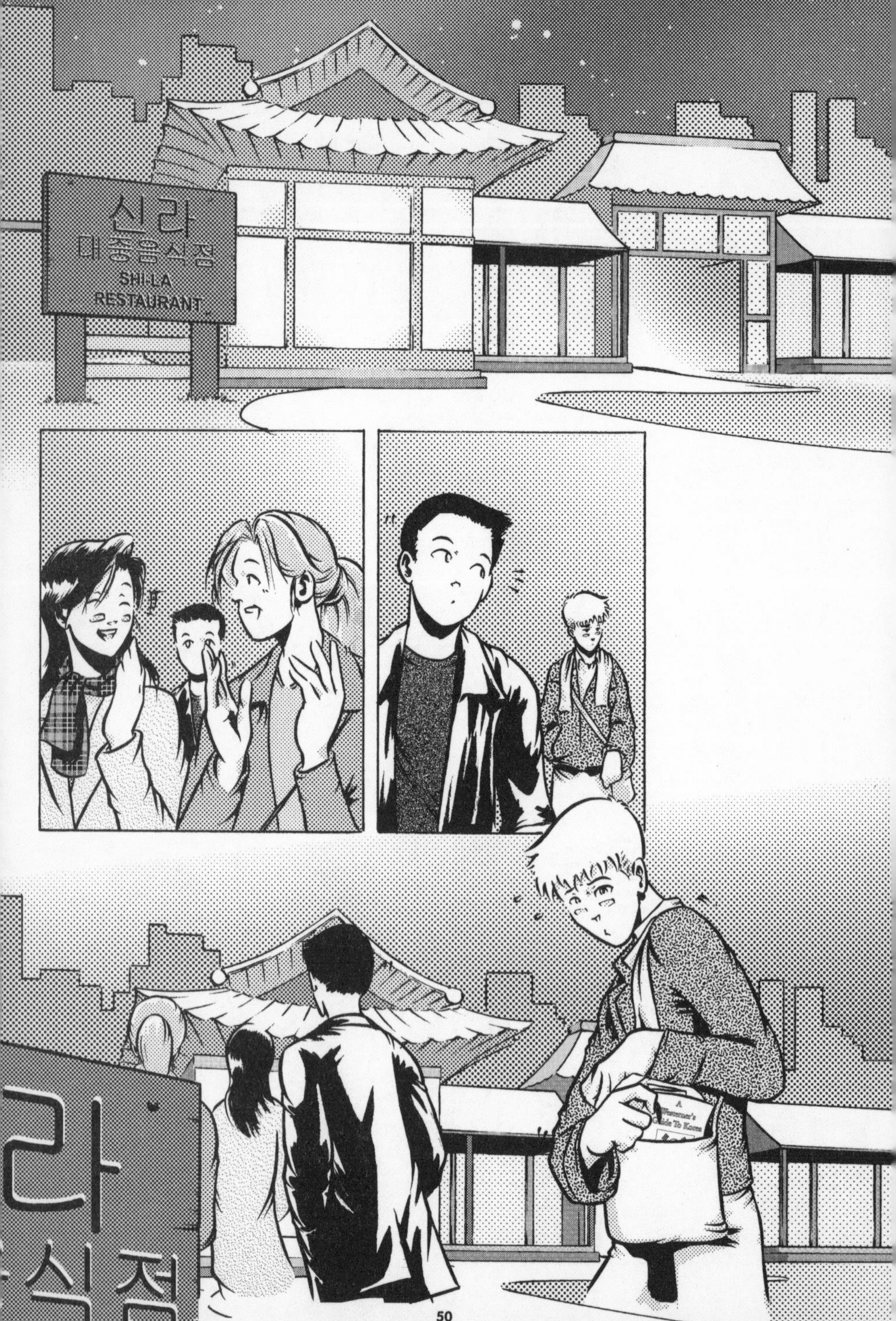
신라
대중음식점
SHI-LA
RESTAURANT
A Westerner's Guide To Korea
라
식점

Chapter 13

SHI-LA ME, SHI-LA ME NOT

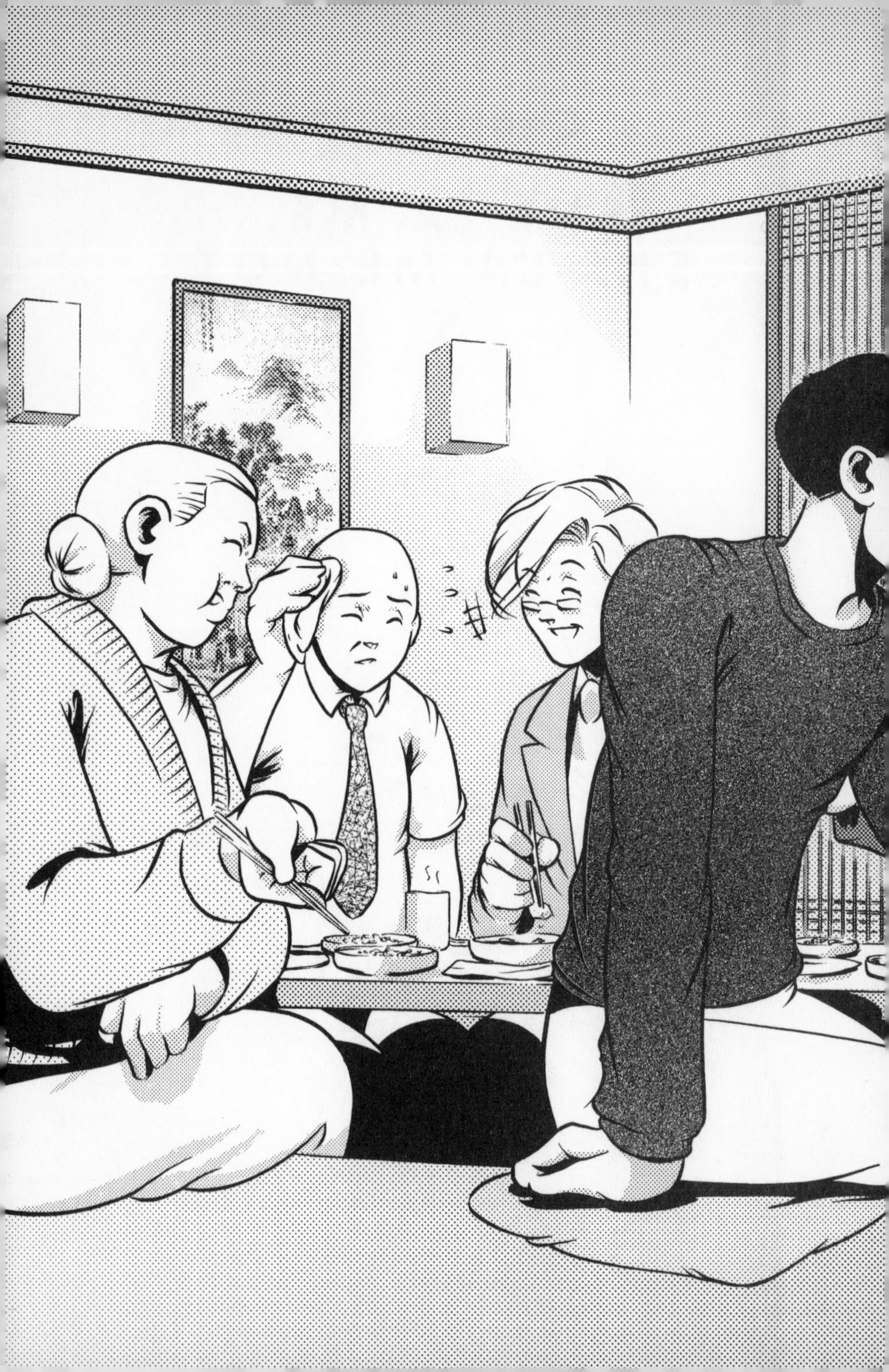

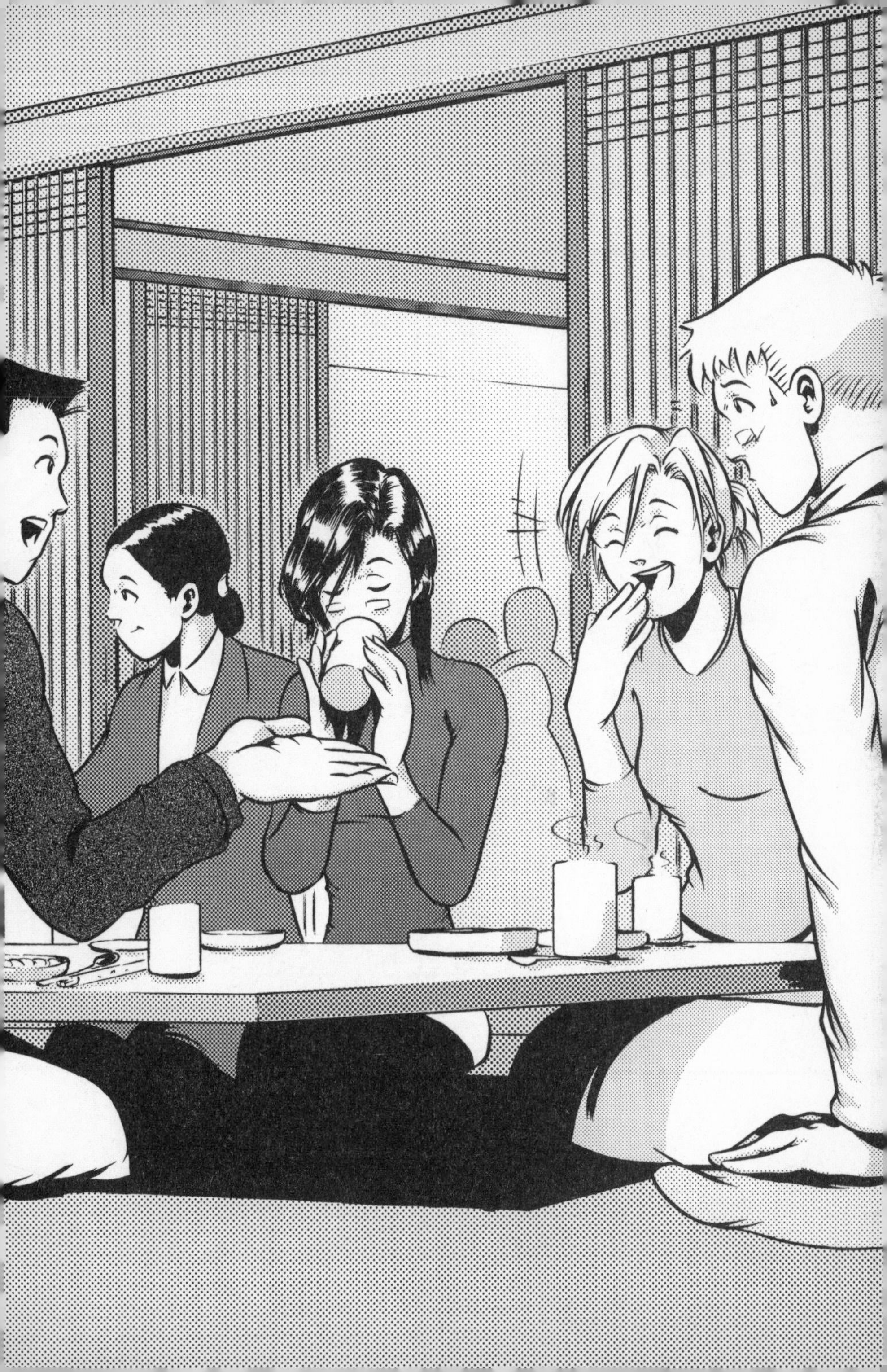

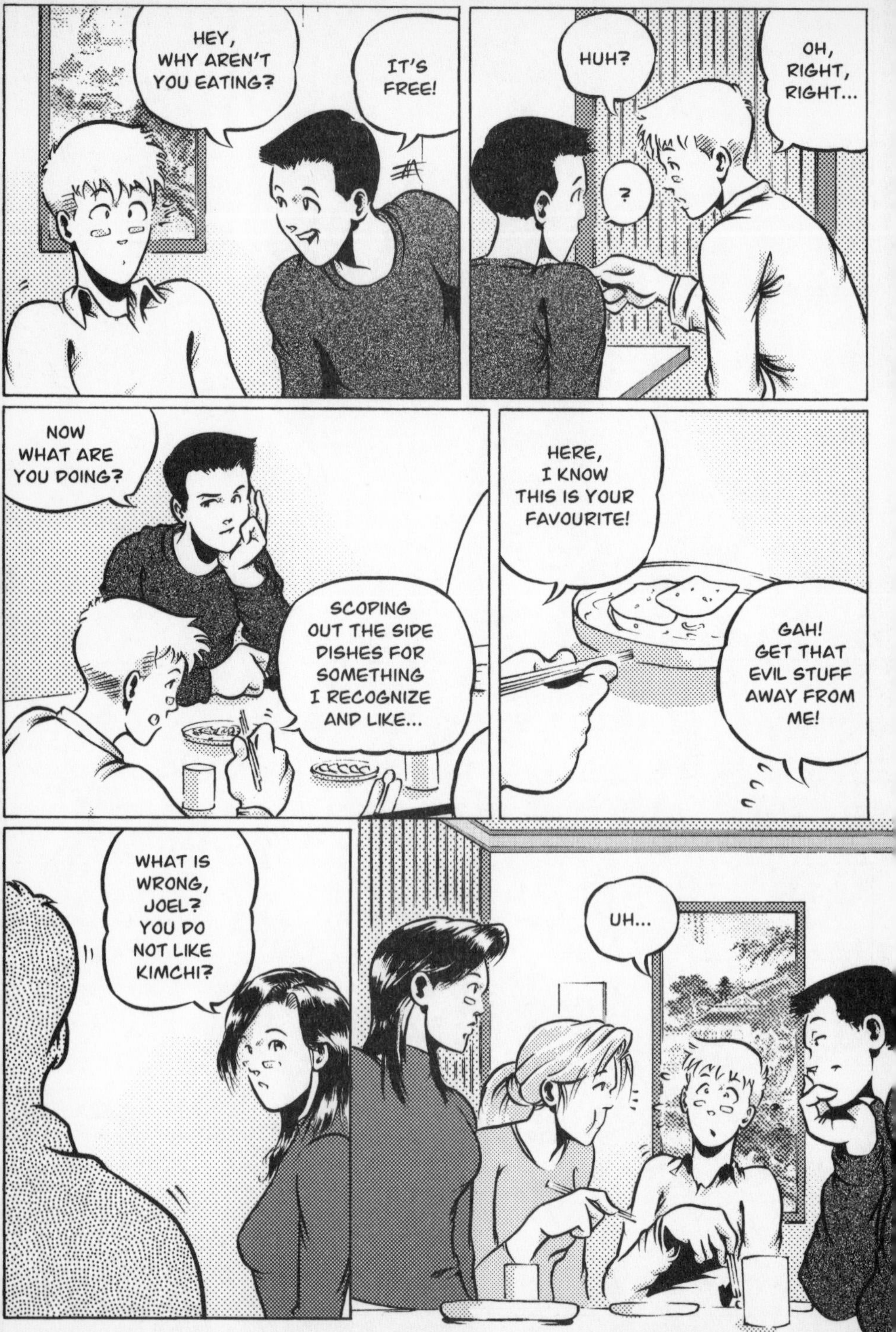
HEY, WHY AREN'T YOU EATING?
IT'S FREE!
HUH?
OH, RIGHT, RIGHT...
?
NOW WHAT ARE YOU DOING?
SCOPING OUT THE SIDE DISHES FOR SOMETHING I RECOGNIZE AND LIKE...
HERE, I KNOW THIS IS YOUR FAVOURITE!
GAH! GET THAT EVIL STUFF AWAY FROM ME!
WHAT IS WRONG, JOEL? YOU DO NOT LIKE KIMCHI?
UH...

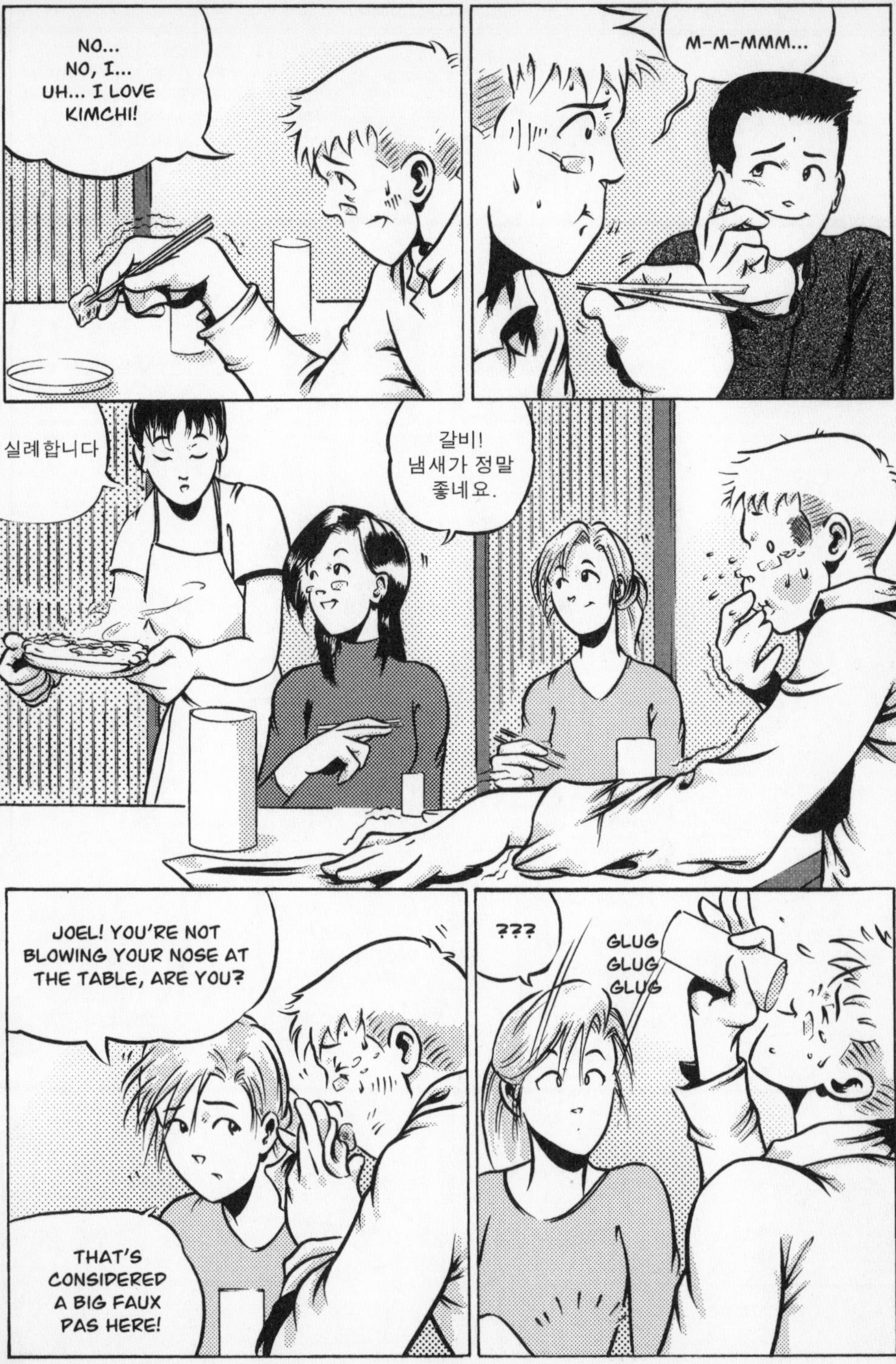
NO...
NO, I...
UH... I LOVE
KIMCHI!
M-M-MMM...
실례합니다
갈비!
냄새가 정말
좋네요.
JOEL! YOU'RE NOT
BLOWING YOUR NOSE AT
THE TABLE, ARE YOU?
THAT'S
CONSIDERED
A BIG FAUX
PAS HERE!
???
GLUG
GLUG
GLUG

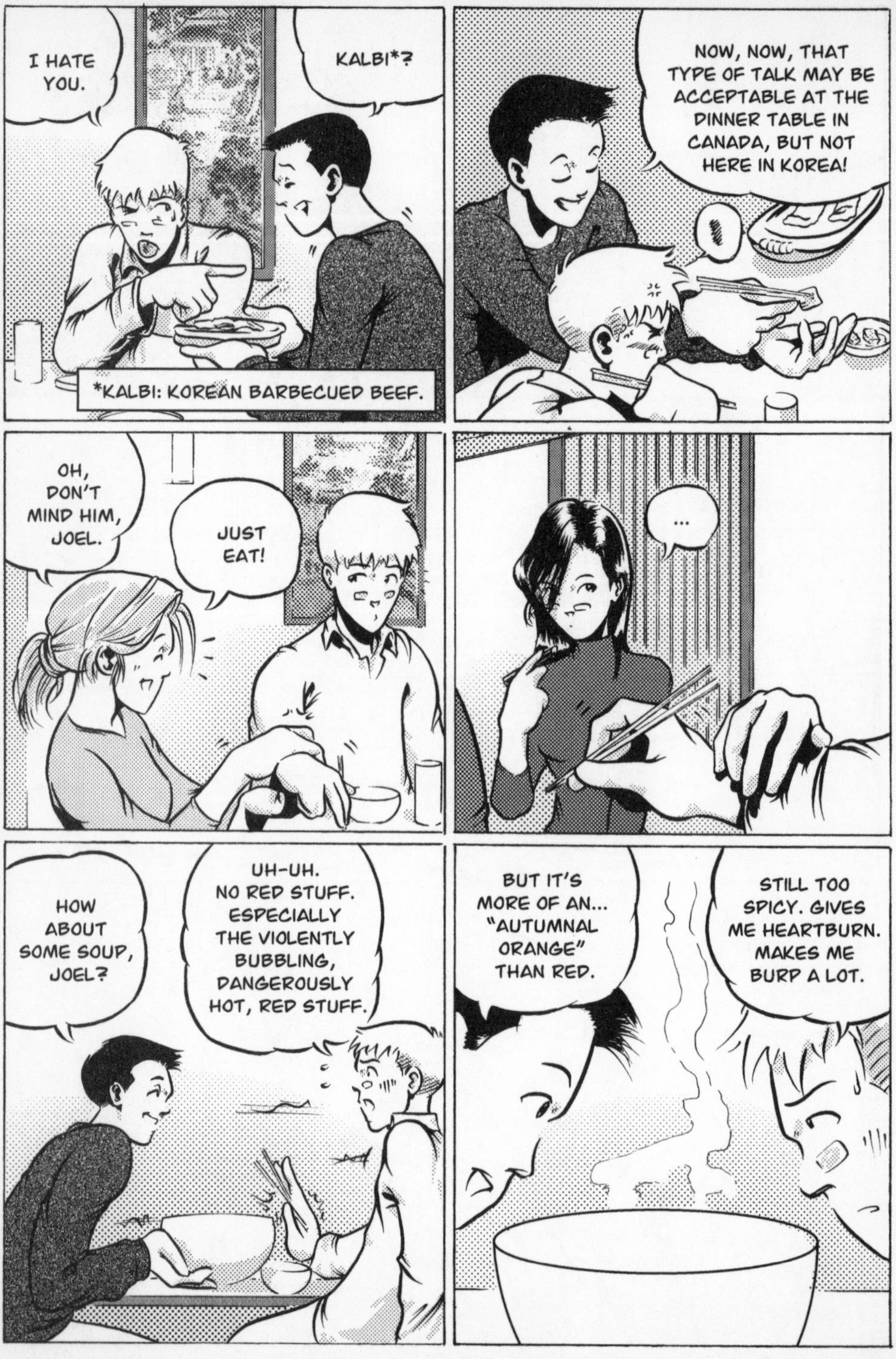
I HATE YOU.
KALBI*?
*KALBI: KOREAN BARBECUED BEEF.
NOW, NOW, THAT TYPE OF TALK MAY BE ACCEPTABLE AT THE DINNER TABLE IN CANADA, BUT NOT HERE IN KOREA!
OH, DON'T MIND HIM, JOEL.
JUST EAT!
...
HOW ABOUT SOME SOUP, JOEL?
UH-UH. NO RED STUFF. ESPECIALLY THE VIOLENTLY BUBBLING, DANGEROUSLY HOT, RED STUFF.
BUT IT'S MORE OF AN... "AUTUMNAL ORANGE" THAN RED.
STILL TOO SPICY. GIVES ME HEARTBURN. MAKES ME BURP A LOT.

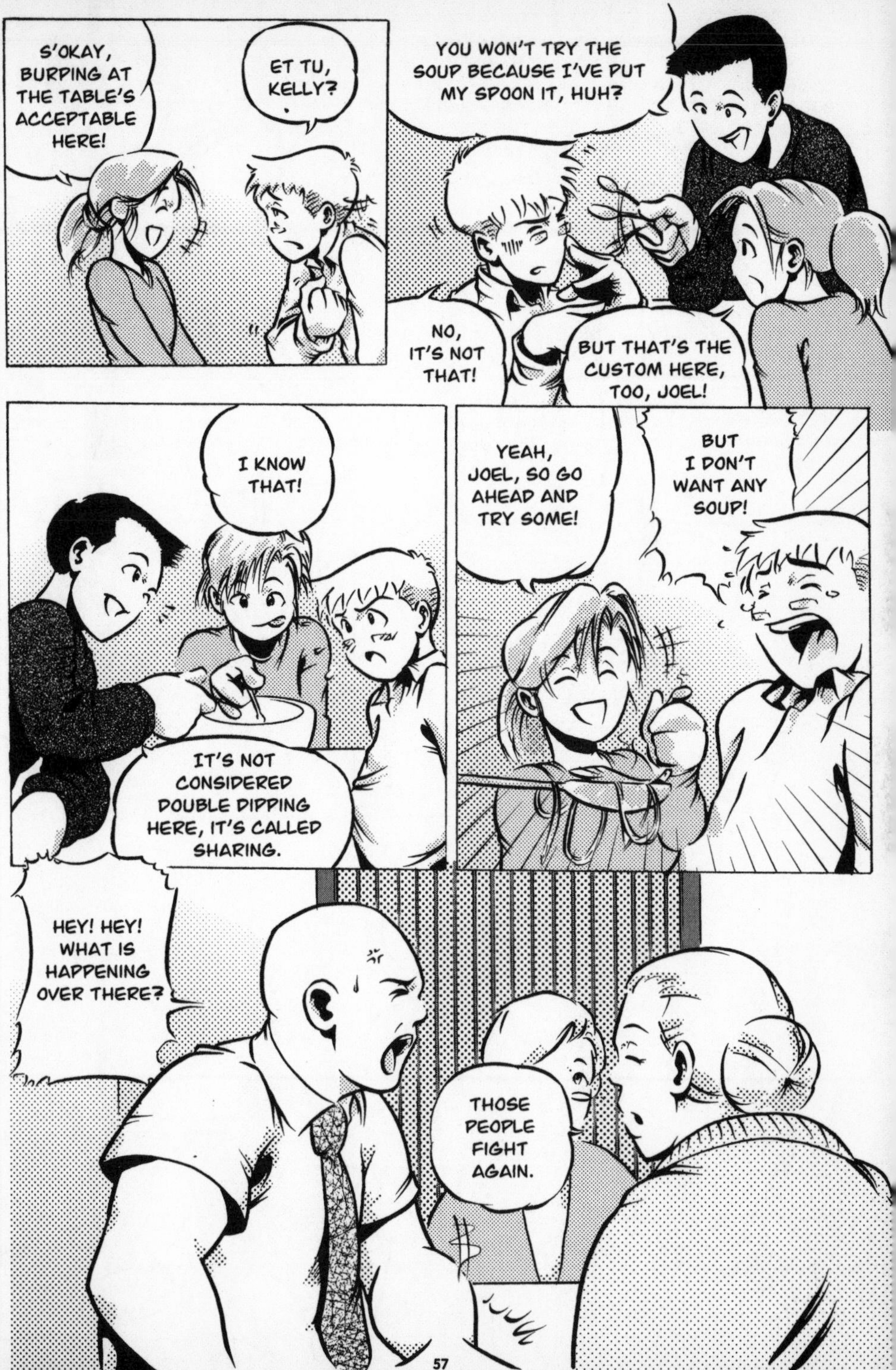
S'OKAY, BURPING AT THE TABLE'S ACCEPTABLE HERE!
ET TU, KELLY?
YOU WON'T TRY THE SOUP BECAUSE I'VE PUT MY SPOON IT, HUH?
NO, IT'S NOT THAT!
BUT THAT'S THE CUSTOM HERE, TOO, JOEL!
I KNOW THAT!
IT'S NOT CONSIDERED DOUBLE DIPPING HERE, IT'S CALLED SHARING.
YEAH, JOEL, SO GO AHEAD AND TRY SOME!
BUT I DON'T WANT ANY SOUP!
HEY! HEY! WHAT IS HAPPENING OVER THERE?
THOSE PEOPLE FIGHT AGAIN.

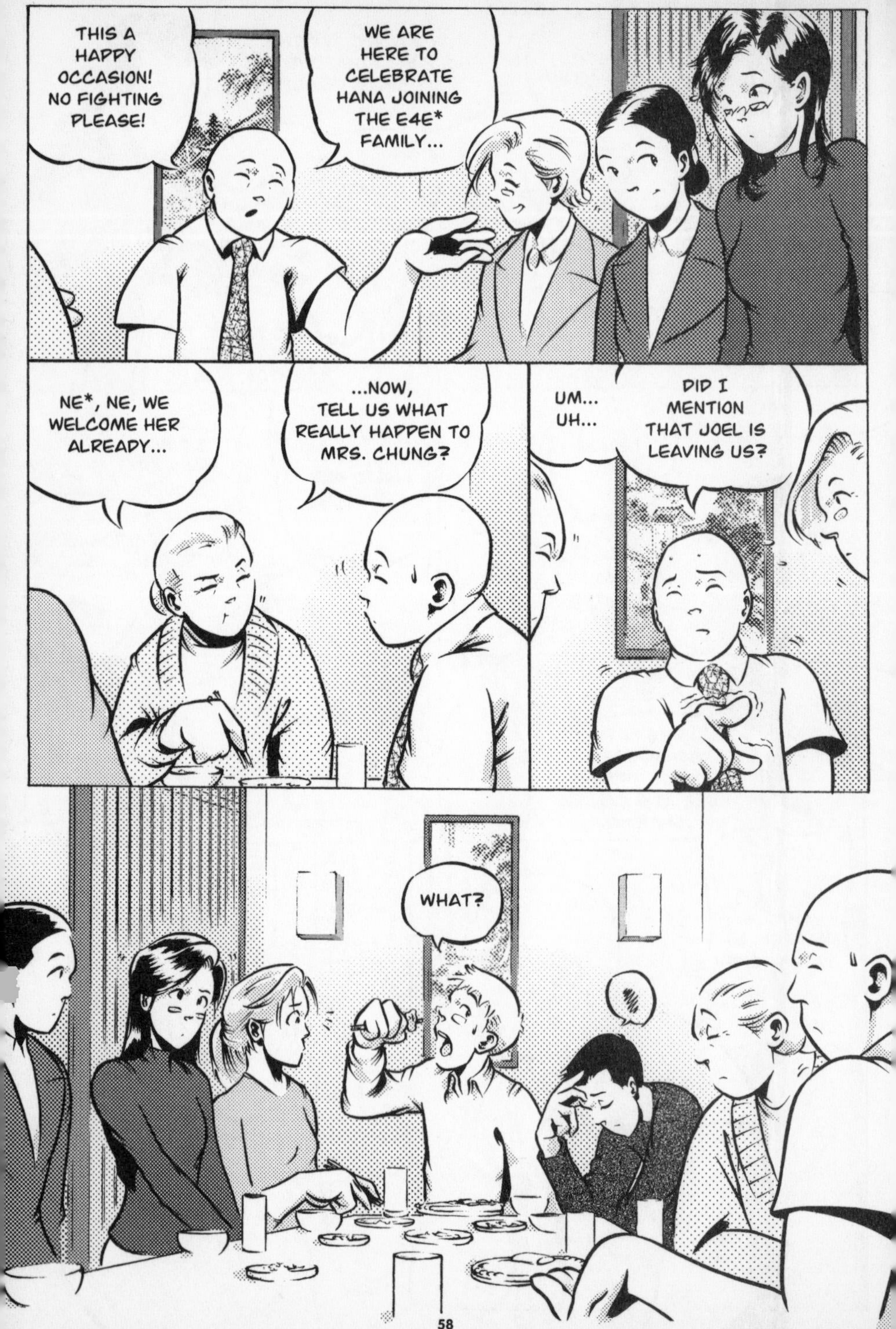
THIS A HAPPY OCCASION! NO FIGHTING PLEASE!
WE ARE HERE TO CELEBRATE HANA JOINING THE E4E* FAMILY...
NE*, NE, WE WELCOME HER ALREADY...
...NOW, TELL US WHAT REALLY HAPPEN TO MRS. CHUNG?
UM... UH...
DID I MENTION THAT JOEL IS LEAVING US?
WHAT?

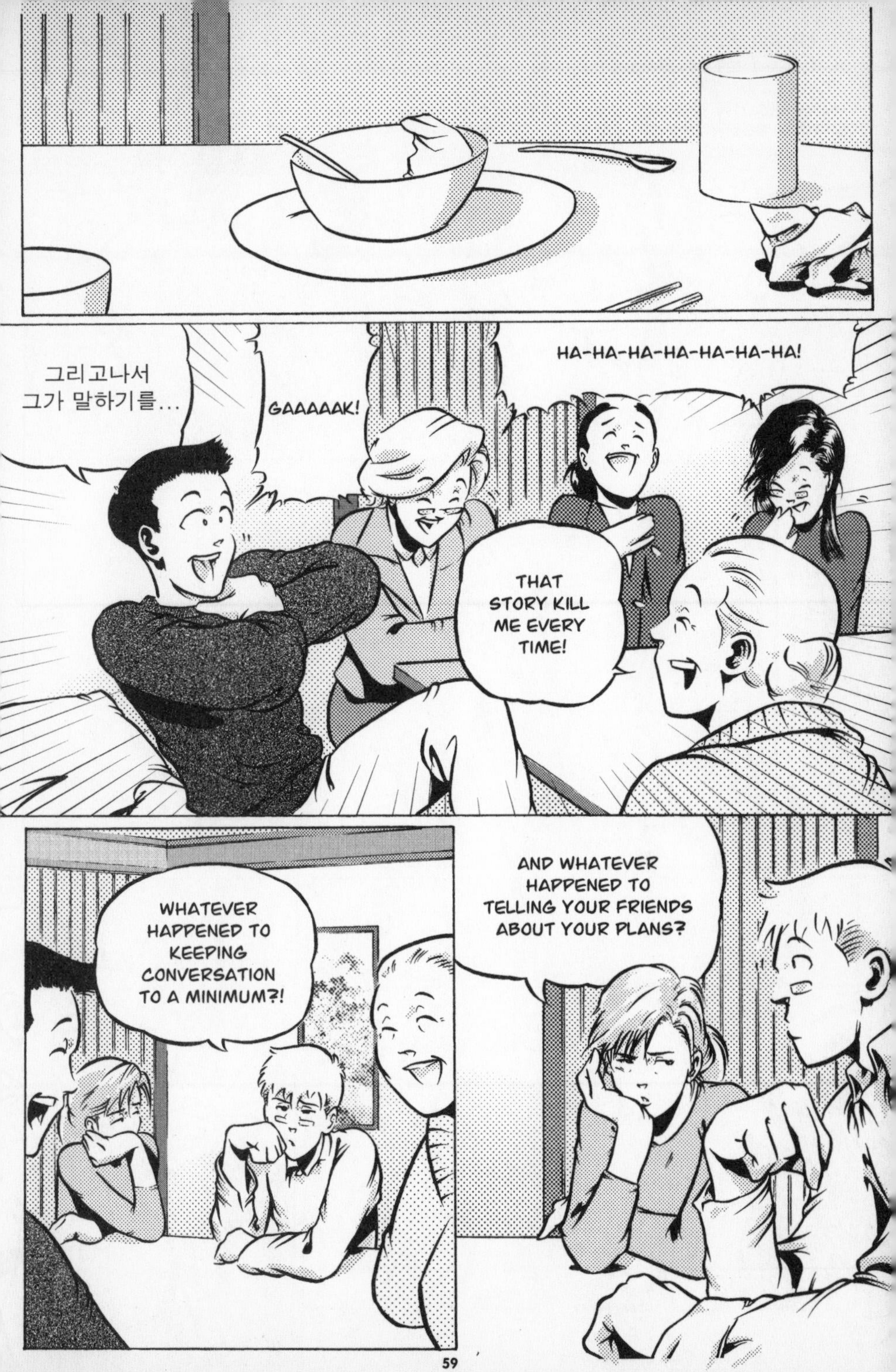
그리고나서
그가 말하기를...
GAAAAAK!
HA-HA-HA-HA-HA-HA-HA!
THAT STORY KILL ME EVERY TIME!
WHATEVER HAPPENED TO KEEPING CONVERSATION TO A MINIMUM?!
AND WHATEVER HAPPENED TO TELLING YOUR FRIENDS ABOUT YOUR PLANS?

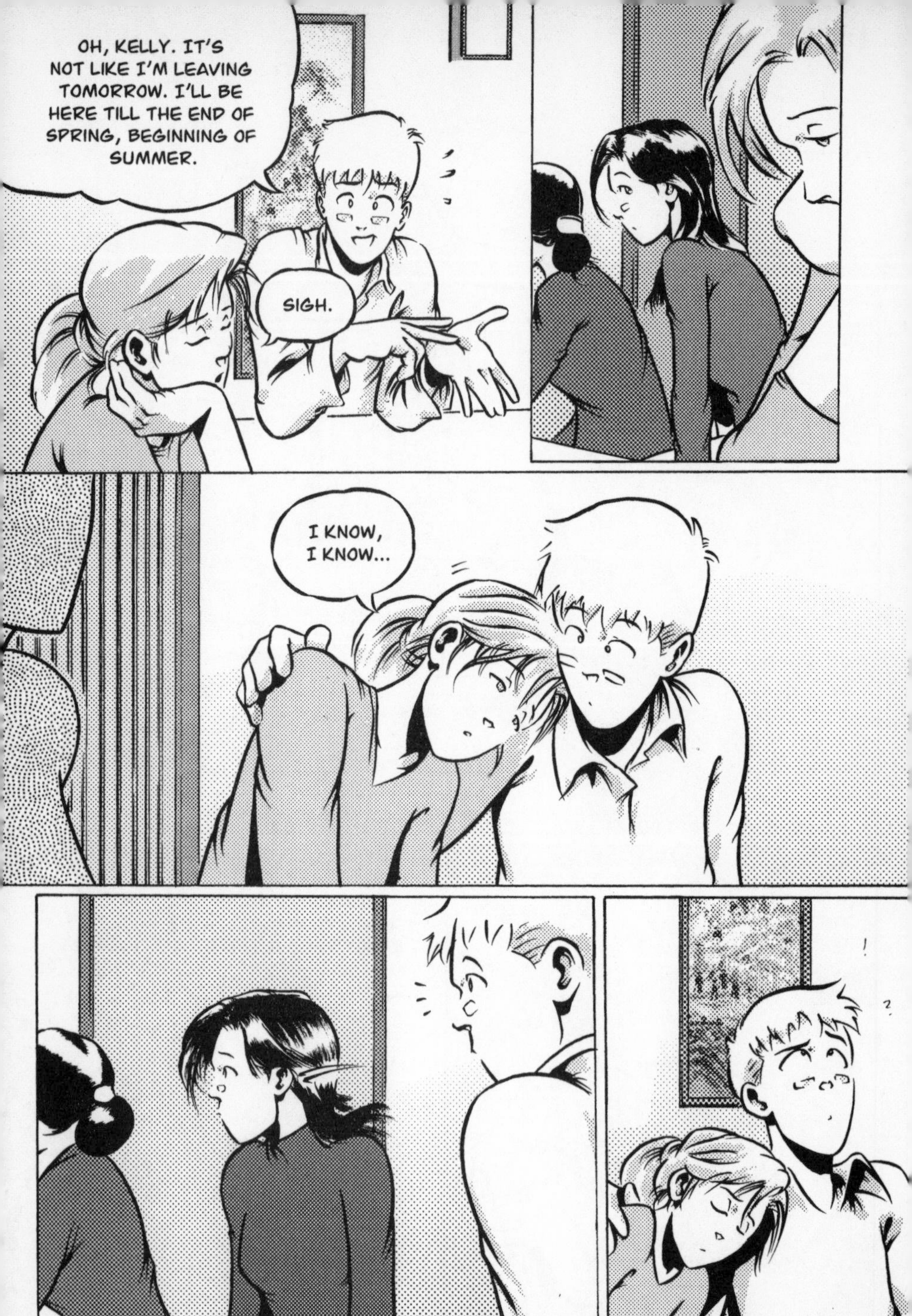
OH, KELLY. IT'S NOT LIKE I'M LEAVING TOMORROW. I'LL BE HERE TILL THE END OF SPRING, BEGINNING OF SUMMER.
SIGH.
I KNOW, I KNOW...
!
?

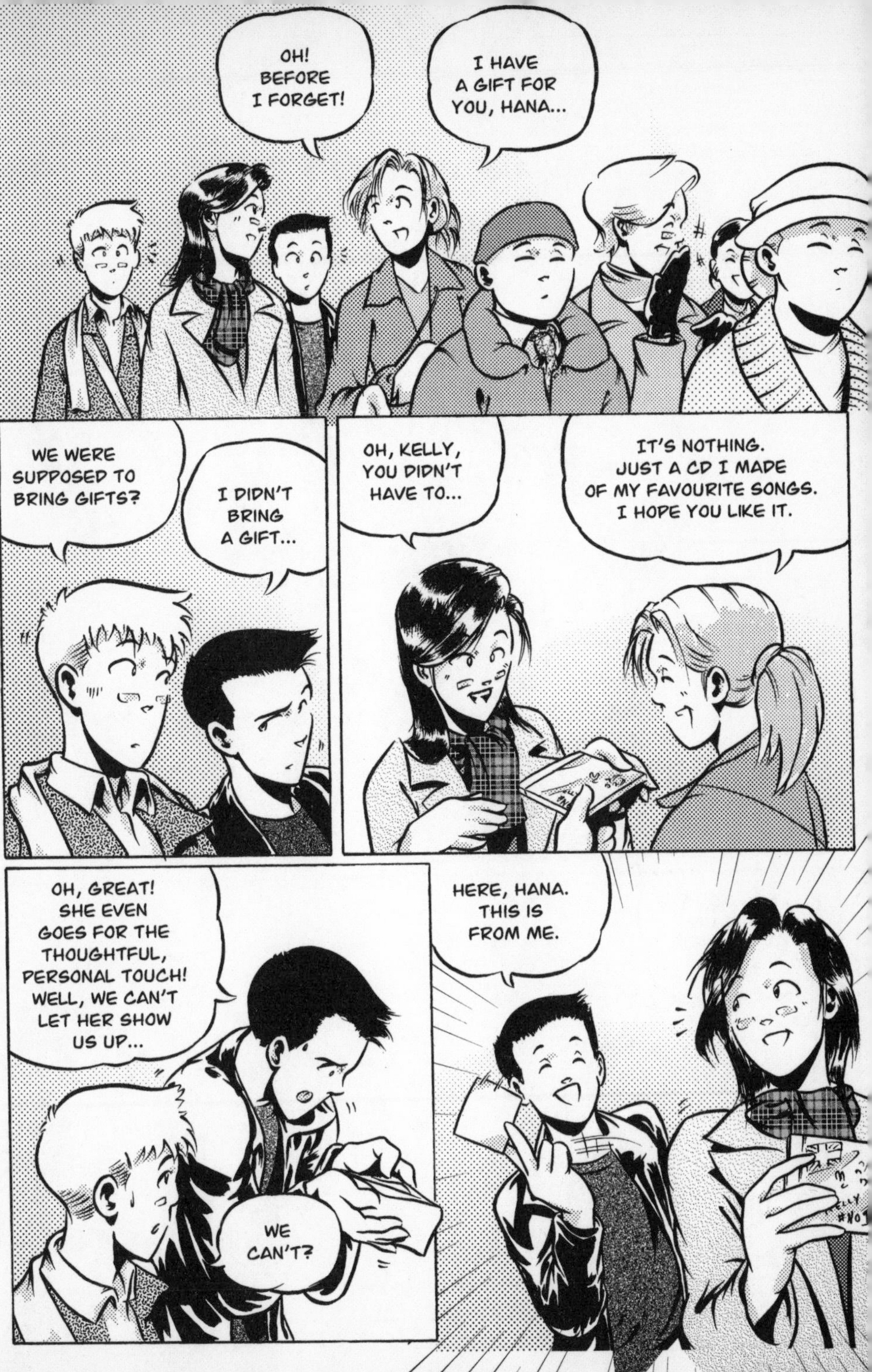
OH! BEFORE I FORGET!
I HAVE A GIFT FOR YOU, HANA...
WE WERE SUPPOSED TO BRING GIFTS?
I DIDN'T BRING A GIFT...
OH, KELLY, YOU DIDN'T HAVE TO...
IT'S NOTHING. JUST A CD I MADE OF MY FAVOURITE SONGS. I HOPE YOU LIKE IT.
OH, GREAT! SHE EVEN GOES FOR THE THOUGHTFUL, PERSONAL TOUCH! WELL, WE CAN'T LET HER SHOW US UP...
WE CAN'T?
HERE, HANA. THIS IS FROM ME.

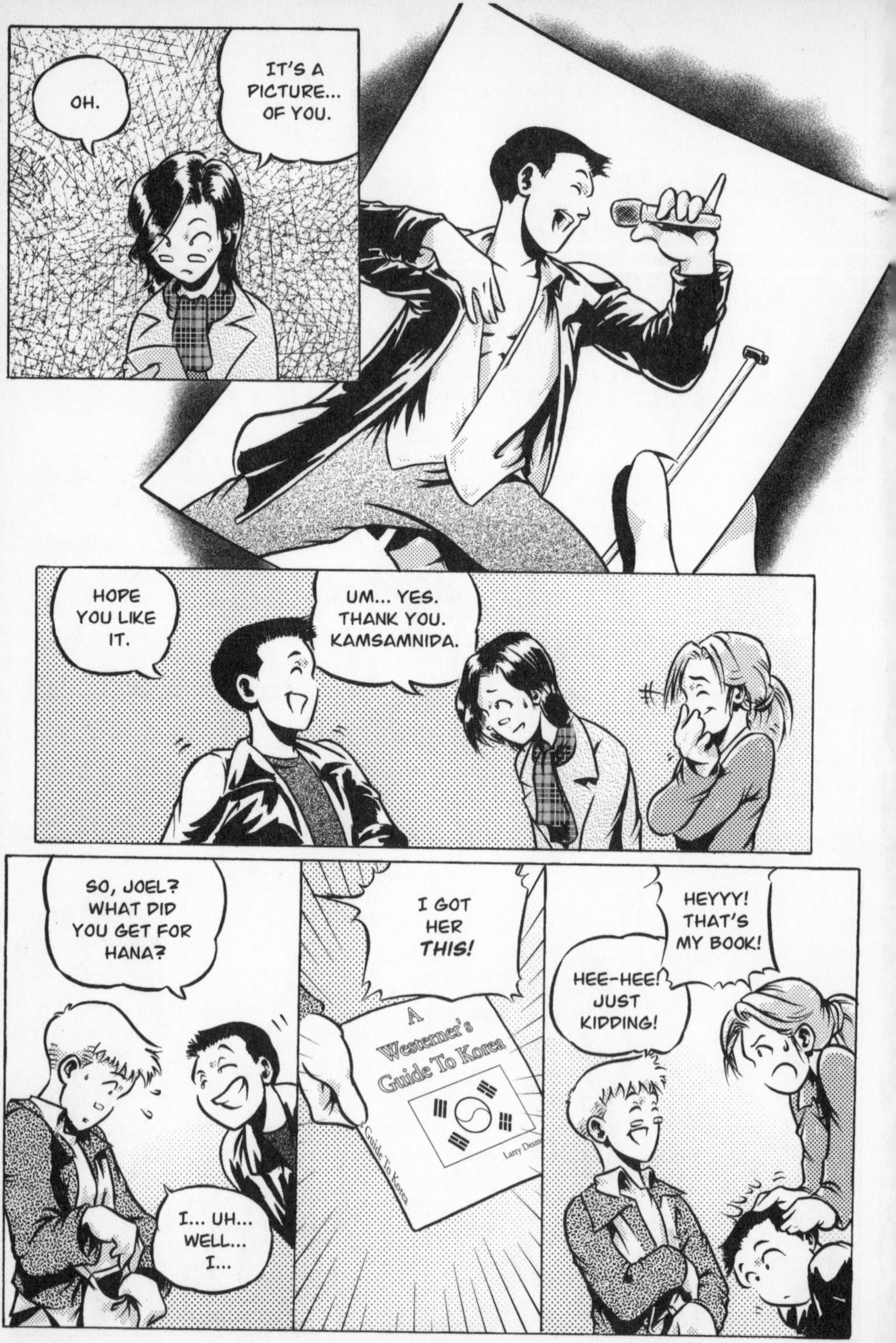
OH.
IT'S A PICTURE... OF YOU.
HOPE YOU LIKE IT.
UM... YES. THANK YOU. KAMSAMNIDA.
SO, JOEL? WHAT DID YOU GET FOR HANA?
I... UH... WELL... I...
I GOT HER THIS!
A Westerner's Guide To Korea
Guide To Korea
HEYYY! THAT'S MY BOOK!
HEE-HEE! JUST KIDDING!

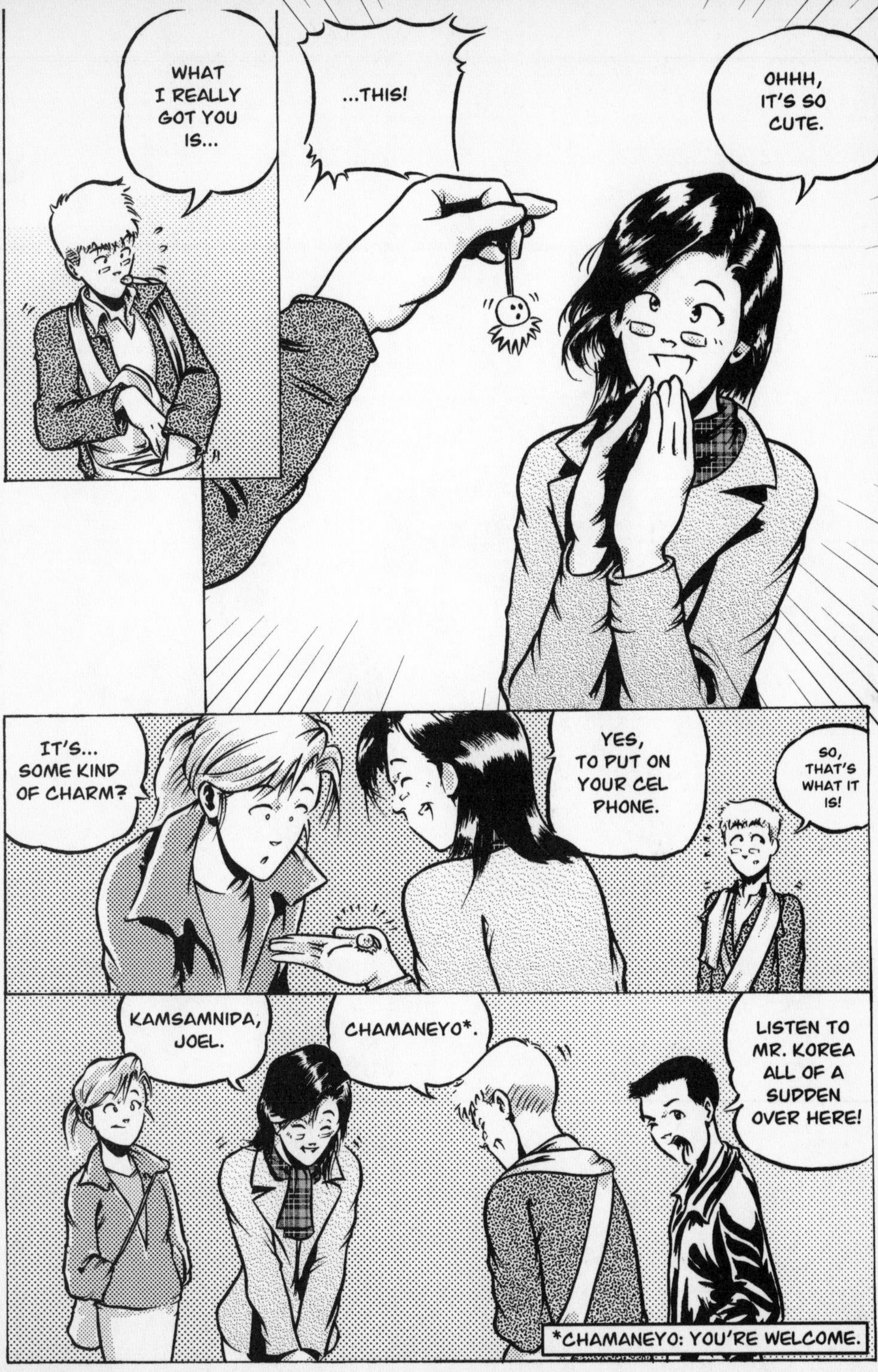

WHAT I REALLY GOT YOU IS...
...THIS!
OHHH, IT'S SO CUTE.
IT'S... SOME KIND OF CHARM?
YES, TO PUT ON YOUR CEL PHONE.
SO, THAT'S WHAT IT IS!
KAMSAMNIDA, JOEL.
CHAMANEYO*.
LISTEN TO MR. KOREA ALL OF A SUDDEN OVER HERE!
*CHAMANEYO: YOU'RE WELCOME.

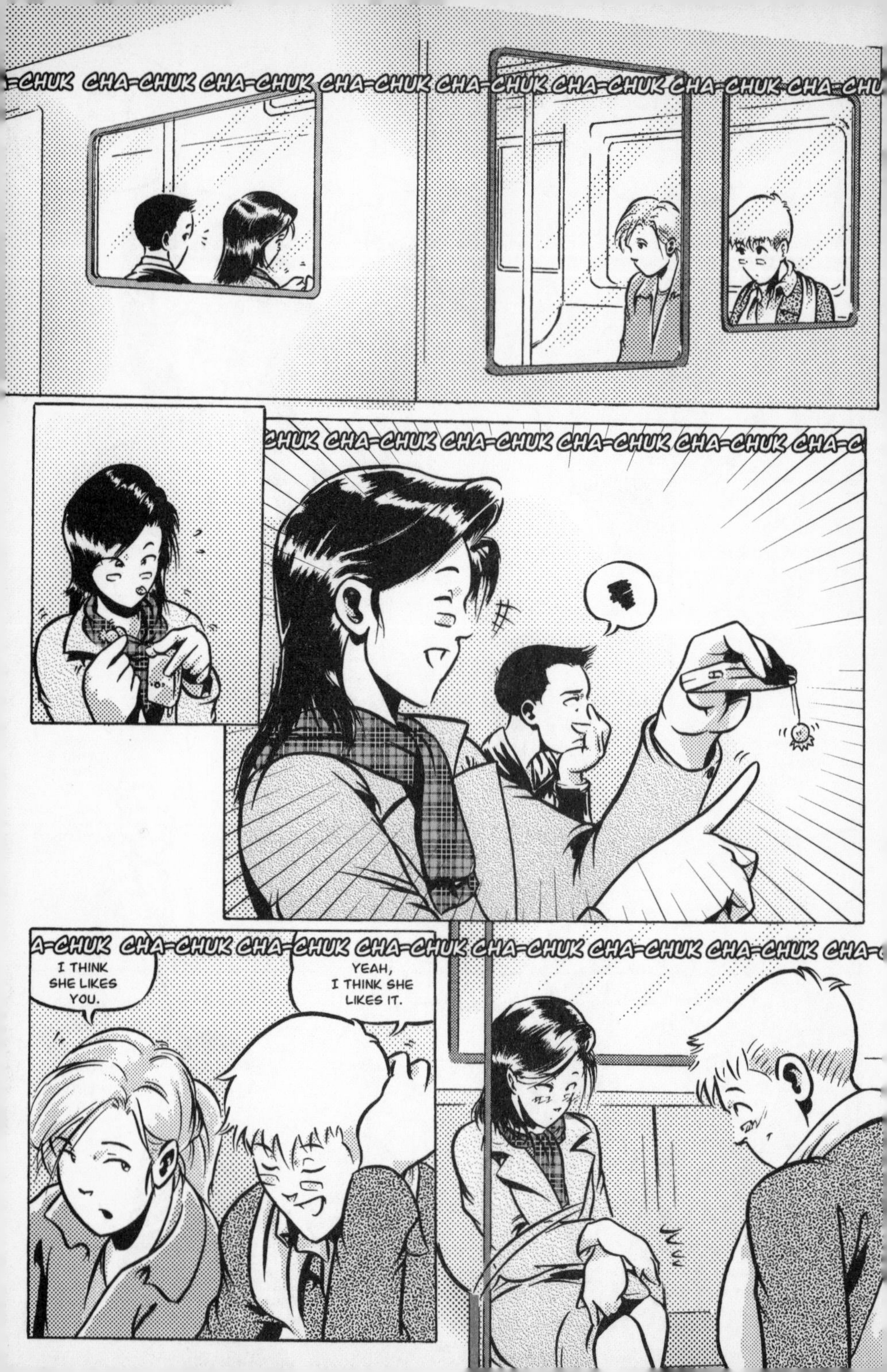
CHA-CHUK CHA-CHUK CHA-CHUK CHA-CHUK CHA-CHUK CHA-CHUK CHA-CHU
CHUK CHA-CHUK CHA-CHUK CHA-CHUK CHA-C
CHA-CHUK CHA-CHUK CHA-CHUK CHA-CHUK CHA-CHUK CHA-CHUK CHA-
I THINK SHE LIKES YOU.
YEAH, I THINK SHE LIKES IT.

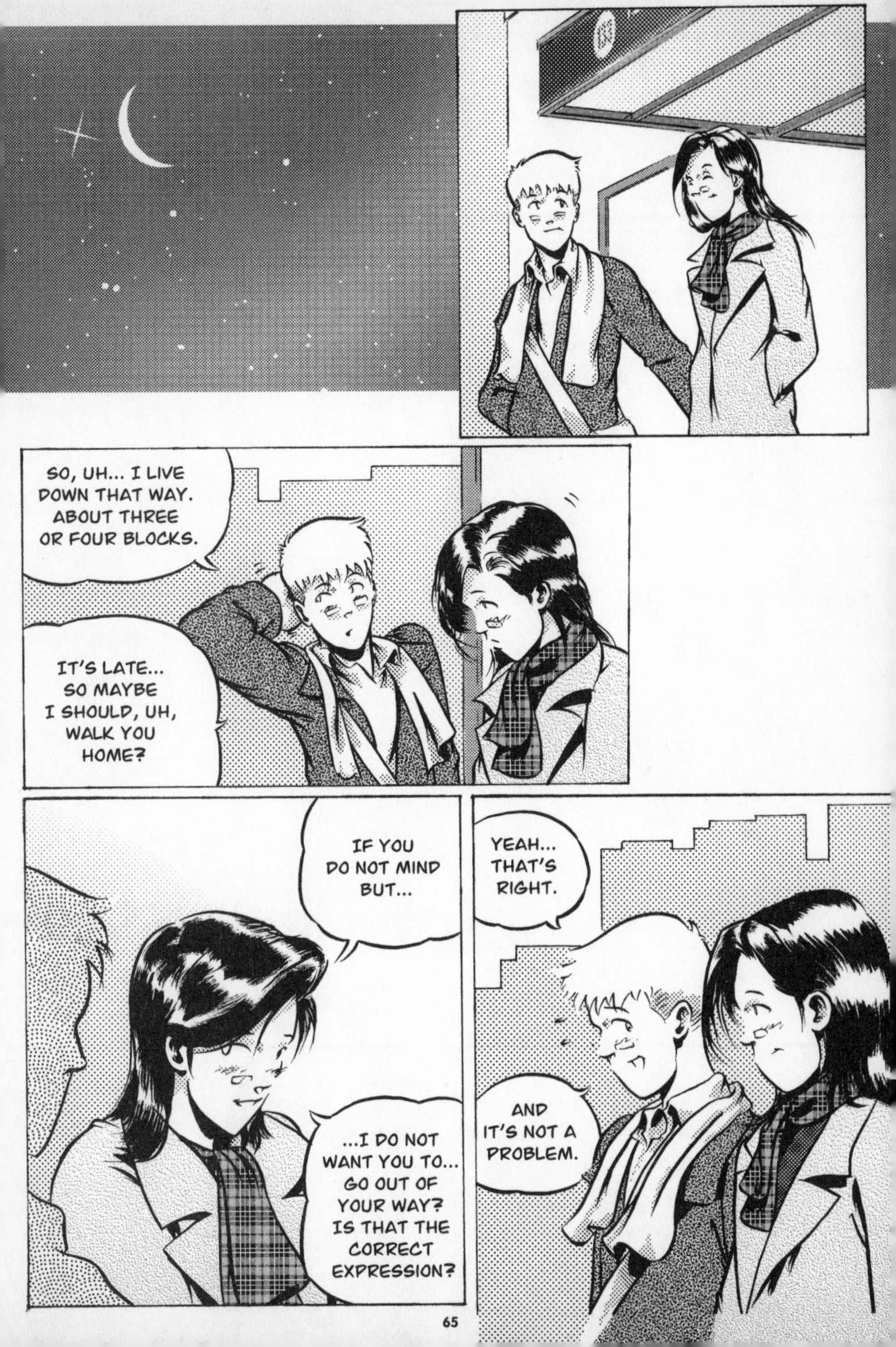
SO, UH... I LIVE DOWN THAT WAY. ABOUT THREE OR FOUR BLOCKS.
IT'S LATE... SO MAYBE I SHOULD, UH, WALK YOU HOME?
IF YOU DO NOT MIND BUT...
...I DO NOT WANT YOU TO... GO OUT OF YOUR WAY? IS THAT THE CORRECT EXPRESSION?
YEAH... THAT'S RIGHT.
AND IT'S NOT A PROBLEM.

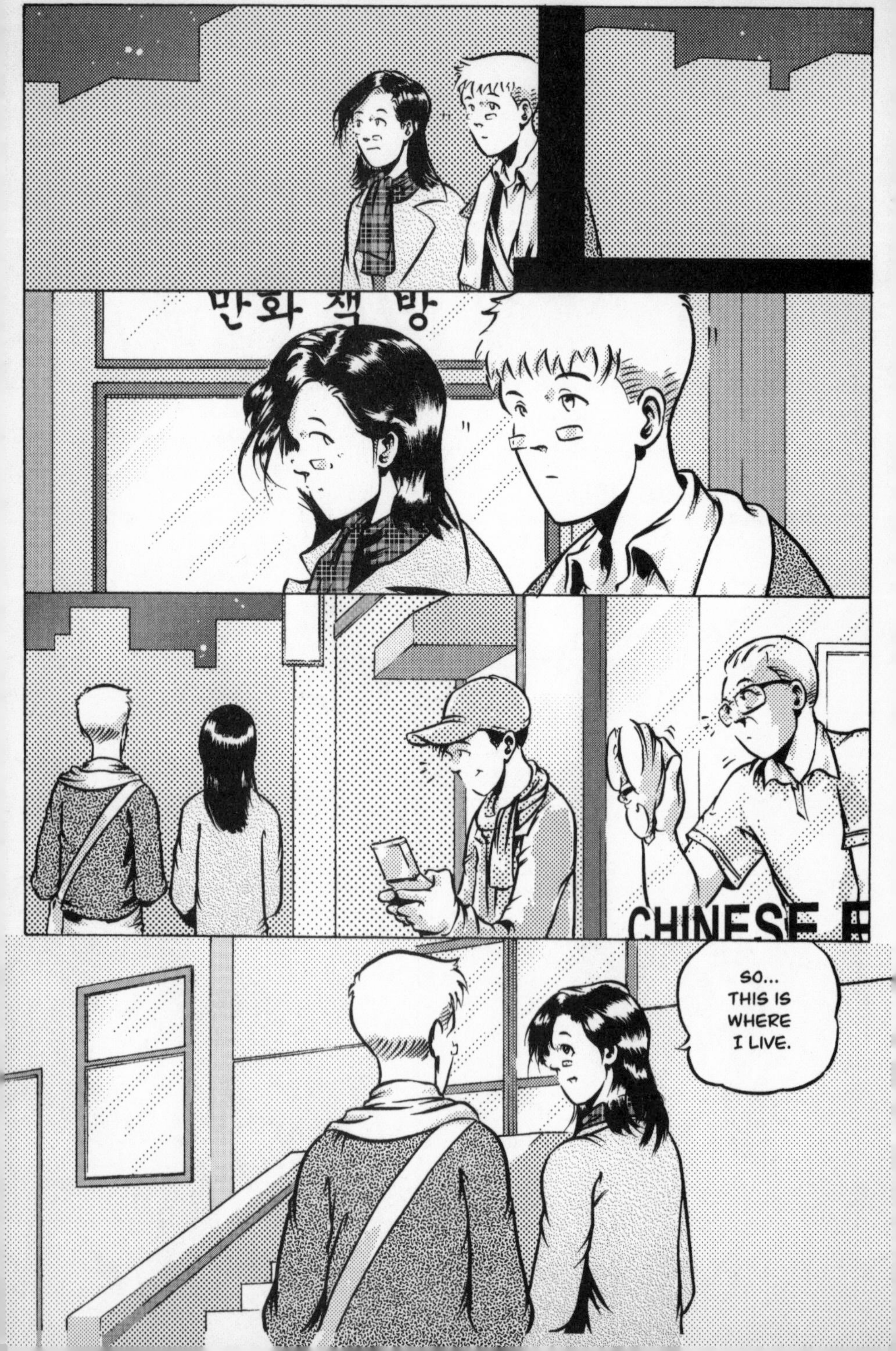
만화 책 방
CHINESE
SO... THIS IS WHERE I LIVE.

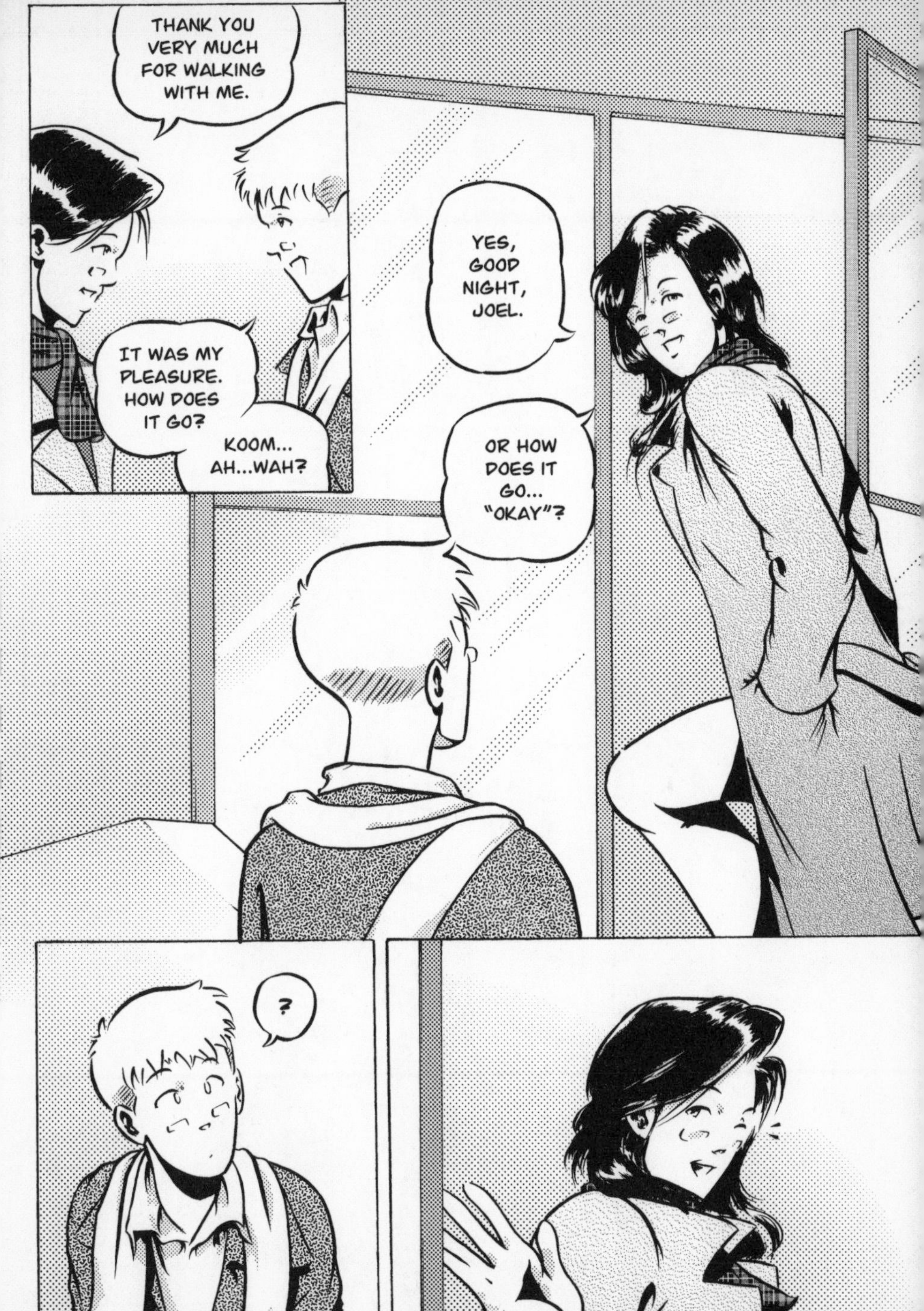
THANK YOU VERY MUCH FOR WALKING WITH ME.
IT WAS MY PLEASURE. HOW DOES IT GO?
KOOM... AH...WAH?
YES, GOOD NIGHT, JOEL.
OR HOW DOES IT GO... "OKAY"?
?

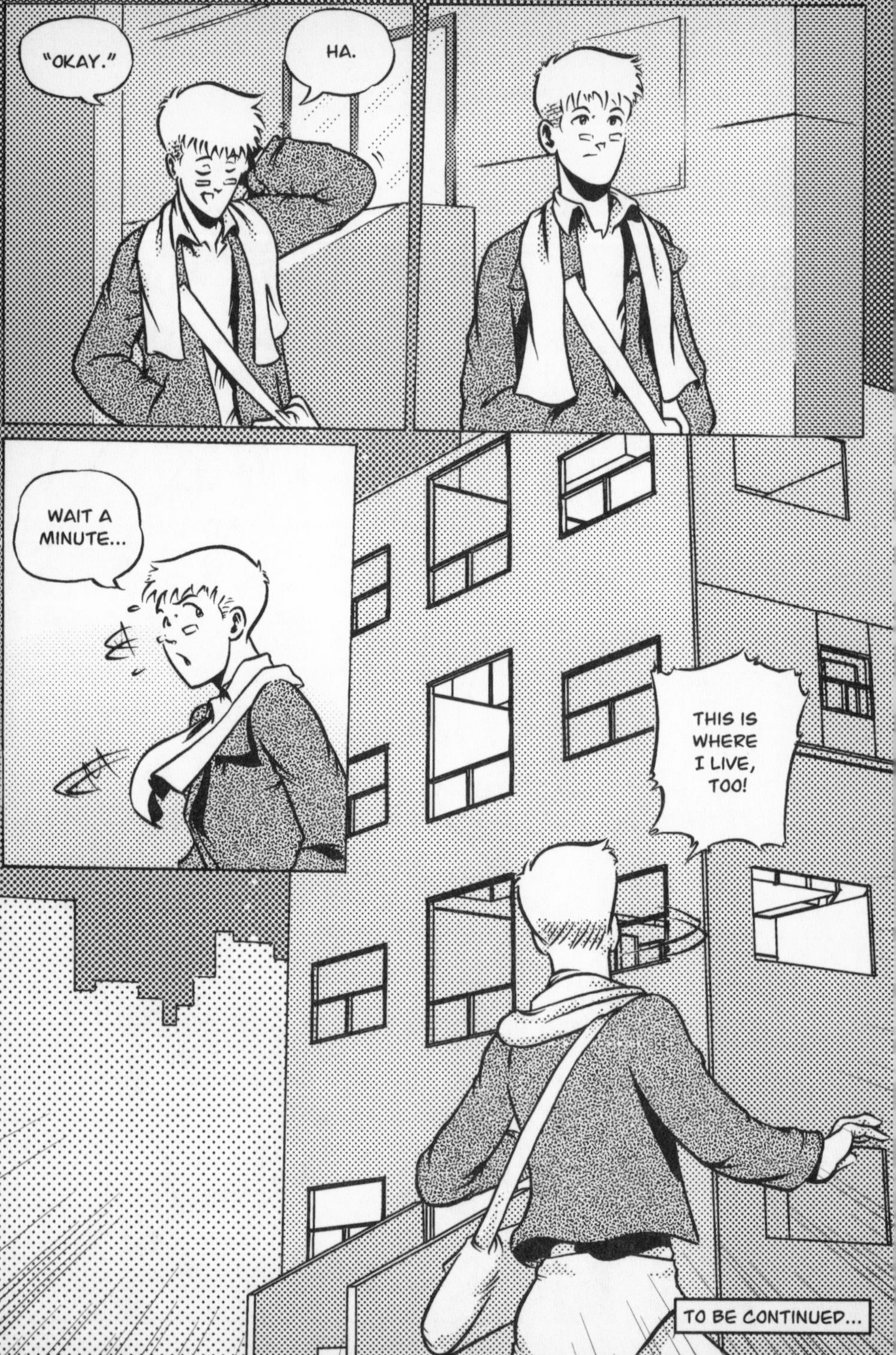
"OKAY."
HA.
WAIT A MINUTE...
THIS IS WHERE I LIVE, TOO!
TO BE CONTINUED...